ANSWERS

FROM A

HIGHER CONSCIOUSNESS

Messages from The Universal Power of Love

Received words

By Alice May Shield

Published by Amaranth Publishing

www.findingthewayofpeace.com

First edition

Published by Amaranth Publishing, 2013

ISBN 978-0-9926682-0-4

A CIP catalogue record for this publication is available from the
British Library.

Printed in the UK on FSC Certified paper which is lead free, acid
free, from well managed forests and Certified by the Forest
Stewardship Council.

The information in this book should not replace diagnosis or
treatment from a qualified medical practitioner for health disorders of
any kind.

DEDICATION

I dedicate this book to all who seek truth.

ACKNOWLEDGEMENTS

My deepest gratitude to Yvonne Tarling and Sally Kincart for the spiritual inspiration they gave me in my earlier years.

I give thanks and appreciation to Myrna Smith for her professionalism in proofreading and her sensitive help in editing. Also to John Turner who rescued me with help in formatting.

I would like to convey my immense gratitude and Love to my parents for giving me such a happy childhood and to my husband for all his Love, patience and support.

I give grateful thanks for this cornucopia of fruits

received from a Higher Consciousness.

My only accomplishment was to open my arms and gather them.

CONTENTS

INTRODUCTION

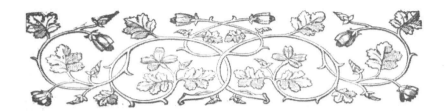

Introduction

For years I had wielded my atheist beliefs like Britannia's shield before me. Then one day in 1981 I attended a meditation class which set in motion a series of life-changing events. Having two demanding jobs, a fourteen-month old child and another on the way, I felt I needed something to relieve the stress in my life. I thought I would sneak in at the back of the room and assess if the meditation was what I wanted. To my dismay it was a small group so I could not be anonymous and, horror of horrors, it looked as if it were religious. There was a photograph of an Indian guru on an altar and food was placed in front of it.

I sat for a few minutes and, wanting to avoid anything religious, I got up to leave. The leader of the group followed me to the door and asked me what it was that I was seeking. I suppose that is the million dollar question. I am not quite sure what was said between us but it was her gentleness and her demeanour that stopped me in my tracks. She suggested that I could just sit quietly and find peace in the group. I did.

The second week, although still defensive and questioning, I let down my guard and, as I did so, I noticed that wherever the woman walked, a light went with her.

I was intrigued.

On my way home cycling through a park on the third week, the moon was shining brightly in the starry sky and I marvelled at it. I started to laugh involuntarily. I started to cry and shake. All my emotions mixed up into an outpouring of tears and joy. Then whoosh! Inexplicably, from somewhere, came a *knowing*, without a shadow of doubt, that there was a divine higher power, all-encompassing, all loving and of infinite strength. I felt it envelop me and shatter me into little pieces as if I was everywhere at once. In this unexplainable moment I became aware of every part of creation and the breath, vitality and vibration of all living beings. I felt I was indeed every single little part….. I was the grain of sand, the snake hanging from a bough, the child in her mother's arms, the fish within a shoal, each drop of water within an ocean…..

Time was non-existent throughout this noetic experience until I found myself in a trembling heap on the tarmac path under the trees. I was bathed in a glowing love, shaking, crying and laughing. I do not know to this day how I had dismounted my bike and landed on the floor! Thankfully there was no-one around observing the scene, because how would one explains such a thing? As I eventually climbed shakily back onto my bicycle, I was overwhelmed with the knowing, that from that moment my life would be forever changed.

I tried telling people what had happened but no-one wanted to listen and I felt rejected. I knew there was an infinite benevolent power, but what should I do with that knowledge?

A few weeks later in the meditation group, I was still unsure of quite how to meditate, but was using the time to sit very peacefully, when another life-changing event occurred. The group leader chimed some tiny bells to denote the end of meditation and she and her nine year old daughter silently rose to their feet and sang the most exquisite melody. It felt as if my heart expanded and all barriers to pure beauty melted. It was a perfect moment in eternity.

As their music filled me, I casually glanced over to the door of the room. I must have had a sense of something drawing my attention for, as I looked, there, next to the entrance stood an angel. Its beauty and radiance were overwhelming and I am sure my jaw slowly dropped in wonderment. Its tall stature and the sense of strength that it exuded heightened this wonderment. Gold, illuminated sashes crossed its chest and its hair shone golden almost to the shoulders. I say 'it' because to me it was neither male nor female. Standing a foot taller than the doorway, it must have been at least seven feet six inches tall and a golden radiance stretched upwards and outwards from each shoulder. The face was beautiful and showed a calm assertion of its power. This being's whole demeanour silently portrayed its capabilities and strength. Long garments reached almost to the floor and the angelic being's hands rested at its sides. It did not turn or alter from its duties which appeared to be of guarding the doorway.

I soaked in this amazing sight, scanning the scene with utter fascination and awe for at least five seconds; my eyes wide open and my wits very much present. Then my logical mind came into action and of course questioned what I was seeing. Disbelief and incredulity came bustling into my mind. With this, the magnificent spectacle of the angel was gone. The doorway appeared empty again. I was choked with emotion which I stifled for the sake of the stillness in the group. My eyes darted around the room searching, longing for another glimpse of the most magnificent sight I have ever seen, but I could see it no longer.

After trying to share these revelations with a very small number of friends and receiving laughter and sniggers, I suppressed my desire to speak of these events, and kept them as a private knowing. I spent the next twenty eight years wondering, "Where do I go from here?" and visiting many faiths, searching for that pure distilled essence which flavoured them; seeking the nectar of all.

In 2006 I made a decision that, instead of seeking truth in a flimsy half-hearted way as I had done almost all my life, I would become dedicated to my seeking and use every quiet moment for this purpose. Not long after making this decision to go deeper, to seek further into truth, I experienced a sequence of vivid dreams full of intense colour and life. This rather peculiar dream I managed to write down.

Dream

I was driving a train over rocky ground, around sharp bends and steep hills. I was also entertaining and providing care and sustenance for many people on the train.

Then I sat down to rest and was asked, "What is the most important thing to you?" Feeling newborn and naked, I answered, "Seeking love and approval all my life and then realising we have always been loved."

I settled down to eat, full of happiness and expectation. There were two of us sitting at the same table and the other person received a whole round melon on a plate. I received just a stalk which surprised me. I then became aware that, just as the stalk is the connection to the whole juicy melon, the stalk that I had received could also be symbolically a connection to knowledge, truth and totality.

Full of vitality, I felt that I could do anything! I lifted people up and carried them. It was a celebration. I whizzed and twirled, flew and climbed. I laughed and beamed. Never had I felt so ALIVE.

When I awoke, I carried this aliveness with me all morning in an amazed wonderment, but being presented with the stalk of a melon in my dream made me laugh, and it seemed ludicrous.

Later I seemed to receive clarity on the meaning of the dream. The train represented my life up to this point, serving food to many people being my nursing and therapy work. Sitting down at the table in my dream represented a potential new part of my life when I might be allowed to find peace and receive knowledge and truth.

Then the comical stalk actually took on full meaning, representing me being given the link; the communication with the completeness and sweetness of truth that I now seek.

I needed that connection; that connection with higher truth.

But how?

Earnest prayer became my focus; not to the concept of God as in compartmentalised, structured religions, but to the Universal Supreme Power that I felt so profoundly when cycling home that night many years before. Religions, I feel, are made by man in order to make sense and structure of a boundless power and infinite love, incomprehensible to our worldly minds.

My praying, my asking, was intense. My longing was like a physical ache. One day I asked, "Please let me feel a connection with Highest Truth. Let me hear you." Because I was particularly tired that day I gave up the fight, gave up the struggle. I surrendered. I physically, literally surrendered. Mentally I visualised giving every tiny part of me over to the source of Love, the Highest Power. I offered even my thoughts to love, light, peace and joy.

In that moment of complete surrender, my head started to rock gently from side to side and almost imperceptibly my body began to sway as sometimes happens in deep prayer. I did not resist; I trusted. The movement slowly stopped and I felt vertigo for a few seconds as my body seemed to be realigned. It felt as if my spine lengthened and as if I was lovingly held.

There was a feeling, a knowing, that some threads of mine were interwoven with a Higher Consciousness. I chanced to ask a question and as words were received I picked up a pen.....

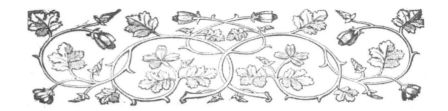

ANSWERS FROM A HIGHER

CONSCIOUSNESS

CHAPTER ONE

THE GARDEN OF LIFE

Alice: "If I am in tune with a Higher Consciousness of Truth, may I ask, what is your priority for my life?"

Higher Consciousness: "To bring you back to your green grass meadow, in the garden of your life. To bring you back to your Peace, which is Oneness with me. All else can blossom from this place."

Alice: "Please tell me more about the garden of life."

Higher Consciousness: "A fruitful garden will always need feeding and the feed for the garden of life is Love.

See Love in everything you do, everything you touch and in everyone around. See yourself full of Love. Where Love is plentiful, beautiful healthy shoots will flourish, with buds and fruit.

Willing insects and birds will pollinate and carry the nectar and pollen far, filling the world with purest life.

By seeing Love everywhere, you will bypass all the little weaknesses and failings and forgive them completely. Forgiveness strengthens and allows more Love to feed everyone and everything. Forgive all the trials and tribulations that you see around you. Forgive, forgive and forgive again."

Alice: "Thank you Higher Consciousness. That is a beautiful metaphor for the whole of life. What would you like me to do now?"

Higher Consciousness: "Just be receptive. Be like a plant in the garden of life. Spread your roots into the earth and your branches and leaves to the sun. Be receptive for what I have to give you. It is here in abundance. Have no fear.

Feel the uptake of the minerals of life flowing through the water in the soil where you stand. These minerals are faith. They will keep you strong and grounded and give good roots. Feel the warmth of the sun on you; this is my Love given in abundance to all. The Love will help you to grow towards the Light, to turn your leaves towards me and to grow around obstacles.

The water falls from above and drenches the soil. It flows though you and back out of your leaves. The water contains and is spirit. The energy of spirit and the purpose of spirit is to move. It encompasses the flow of life. Nothing lives without, and all is of, spirit. Now feel the plant strong in spirit and with the potential to bloom. This is how everyone is and this is how I see everyone. I will always nurture you; always.

Be in Peace."

I began dedicating most of each morning to meditation and reaching that place of complete surrender to Love Source. When asking for communication with a Higher Consciousness, I experienced a transient spinning feeling in my head. If I also visualised Supreme Love connecting with everyone and everything, I instantly felt tapped into a universal power source which seemed to ripple through my body.

After making the decision to seek truth, all manner of unusual experiences in my inner vision and in my body occurred at which I have marvelled. The form of communication I receive is difficult to describe as it is more felt than heard and this feeling is always of complete Love, Peace and Power.

I have reservations about using the word God. It may be fear of ridicule from family, friends and public. It may be concern that the word God has mainly Christian overtones whilst I respect all searching for enlightenment. It may be because I feel that the Supreme-of-All is nameless, infinite; the incorporeal purest existence, neither masculine nor feminine.

Because I do not know which name to use, I hope readers will forgive me when I use different names when I want to communicate with the Highest Love Source.

Alice: "Do we have a task in this life?"

Higher Consciousness: *"You have tasks but you have total free will to carry them out when, where and if you desire."*

Alice: "What are the tasks?"

Higher Consciousness: "The universal tasks are to love and to be loved, to give out your Light and to see Light in everyone and everything."

Alice: "Peculiar things happen to me particularly when I reach towards Highest Love in my meditations. Would you explain some of this?"

Higher Consciousness: "You sometimes feel an energy surge when you link in and then, I will explain in material terms, the transducer effect will protect you from too much energy. You have felt surges before I know, but you will always be protected.

Dear Alice, you are blessed, as everyone is blessed, in the same amount of Love but you are opening up to more communication. This opens up pathways from Highest Love to everyone, not just to you. Just as a diamond has different, beautiful facets which catch the Light but are part of the whole, and the sea is composed of millions of droplets, you are part of one cohesive whole.

The pathways to Truth are there, the links are there, just waiting for people to open and use them with more Love intention.

There is a sea of Love between you and me, with no beginning, no joins, no breaks, just a pure open link. As you begin to swim or fly through this Love to me, at first it may feel thick and turbid as you struggle, dragging you back to the denseness you call your reality. Some people just have the intention of Love and drift and soar with no resistance.

There is nothing stopping anyone linking in directly with Pure Love, only their own resistance.

Your resistance comes from fear. There is never any need for fear. Fear creates the transformer effect to reduce the experience of the full power of Love. You are all pure Love but do not realise it yet. When you realise it completely, you will have no use for the body and will leave the material dream."

Alice: "Various ancient spiritual teachings say we are all one. Now these words I am receiving are also implying that we are all joined, linked, connected in some way, but are we not individuals?

Higher Consciousness: "You think you are all individuals but you are clusters of energy within a circuit of life, all interlinking and communicating knowingly and unknowingly. Just as you are linked with seemingly invisible energy links, that same energy is composed, in your perception, of objects and other people. To put it metaphorically, you are all part of a huge "circuit board" of energy. Nothing and nobody is excluded. People think they are in their own thoughts in their own little world, but really they are part of everyone's dream world. All the thoughts there have ever been are part of a mass consciousness.

You perceive yourselves as separate individuals with a small personal space around you. You believe this is so, therefore that becomes your reality and this perpetuates your feelings of separateness. If you change your perception to knowing you are part of a huge ocean of Love with no boundaries, this will become your reality and feelings of separation will be gone."

Alice: "This all sounds as if a grand master mind-controller has created a huge circuit board of energy."

Higher Consciousness: "The Source of all power is much more than a mind-controller, He/She is a giver of mind freedom so anyone can take their part of mind in any direction and create their life as they will. Of course because each part of mind is linked to the One Mind, each part is very powerful and wherever their mind takes them appears as a powerful reality. If many minds have similar thoughts, especially repeatedly, this will create a particular group 'reality'."

Alice: "Some ancient religions and philosophies say that this material world is not solid and real; it is an illusion. But this is not an easy concept to believe. Now modern physics is also saying that solid matter is not solid matter. I am puzzled about this. Please would you clarify?"

Higher Consciousness: "Alice, God so loved that he gave the wholeness of his mind total freedom to express and explore if it chooses. A part of mind did choose to explore and a chain of thought ensued with all the power of the One Mind. This has led to a feeling of straying away from the beautiful Oneness and a feeling of being separate. This feeling of being separate individuals led to defensiveness and fear. These thoughts became like a bad dream containing good and evil. Whilst experiencing the dream, it feels like reality and the reality of spirit feels like an unreachable dream. But within the dream, many have a longing to return, a battle over fear and a desire ultimately to see the Light again, which is actually always here.

The split away from Oneness never really occurred and is but a thought and where your thoughts are focused determines the whole of your experience.

Every day of your worldly life, you are experiencing an enactment of the prodigal son story; a wandering away from the path of happiness and believing yourselves to be unlovable. Your mind that has been exploring, is a part of God's mind and God's mind is always now. There is no time, only this moment. Everything that you think has ever 'happened' is still now and God's mind has already returned to the oneness.

*Your dream is perceived as prolonged and linear but it is all **now**. Your dream state does not provide you with the* *comprehension of this and your dream appears to offer much evidence against it. It will not be until you fully realise that you are God energy, that full comprehension of everything will be yours and this dream that you look on as a physical world will dissolve."*

Alice: "This cannot be! I must be hearing wrong. This is madness! It's turning the world upside down!"

Higher Consciousness: "Yes, the world is madness and Truth is Truth."

Alice: "You have said that where our thoughts are focused determines the whole of our experience of the world. How can a change of thought change our reality in day to day life?"

Higher Consciousness: "Just as the vibration of molecules changes when heated, and this change of vibration can reach far beyond, your change of perception changes the vibrations through you and beyond you, changing how other people and the environment appear and behave. This is just a way of explaining things so that the 'material world' may understand. If things were explained as seas of consciousness and spiritual gateways that are surpassed at less than a blink of an eye, only a few people may comprehend.

Referring back to the change in molecules, in reality there is no restriction in time and space, therefore any so called 'molecules' in any dimension, can be altered in their vibration just by the intent of a thought pattern. This is how healing can occur, when the thought pattern is unconditional Love and complete forgiveness."

Alice: "But this is so much to comprehend. I shall have to read and re-read this until I begin to understand. This is saying that how we see the world is not reality and that we have only strayed from the reality of Oneness in thought alone!"

Alice: "Should I ask for protection when I surrender completely to Love Source?"

Higher Consciousness: "Only if fear enters your mind will you need to ask for protection and this protection will come in the way of reinforcement of the fact that there is nothing to harm you.

Know that everyone is given perfect strength, perfect completeness, perfect Love and that nothing can take this away or destroy any part of this."

Alice: "If fear enters my head what should I do?"

Higher Consciousness: "Do not entertain fear as a house guest. Do not feed it but recognise it for what it is; wrong perception by your free mind that you have been given. Protection as such is never really necessary and your strength lies in your capability to see the Love in everything and in your trusting in the power of Love.

If there is a belief in harmful forces, then visualisations of a protective field will simply be felt as reassurance because, as I say again, your thoughts become your experience. Any further protection is not required for a mind focused on Love.

Alice: "If our strength lies simply in our capability to see Love in everything, why does it say in the Bible to put on your armour?"

Higher Consciousness: "The perception, then and now, is that some outside force is waiting to attack; some entity or being with a will of its own is marauding the Earth, waiting to pounce. What you are asking is, "Is there a devil; is there consummate evil?" Is this right?"

Alice: "Yes"

Higher Consciousness: "Even in Biblical terms, the devil is depicted as a fallen part of God's creation, which is how you perceive yourselves to be, when choosing thoughts other than from Love.

So called evil thoughts and deeds have no power over mankind. Everyone has full authority within their power to choose Love or fear. If mankind mistakenly chooses to harbour and nurture fear thoughts of evil as being real, then that will become their so called 'reality'.

*The power of choice is **power indeed** and thoughts will play out into your experience, whatever is in your mind.*

*There is no devil creature or being which is separate from yourself, with a separate mind that can do you harm or overrule you. There is only one mind. The only so called 'power' of evil is the power of your mind, which is very powerful, in collaboration with the cumulative focus of the collective mind. Your mind has the power of the Supreme Mind and in its free will it can make choices other than from pure Love. This estranged part of the mind is curious, it is mischievous and it thinks it is separate with a need to protect itself. In this defensiveness it also attacks. This part of the mind that has wandered off the path of Love, that thinks fear and attack thoughts, is **perceiving** and **imagining** instead of seeing.*

When there is true sight there is only Love seen everywhere.

9

This diversion away from Truth has also fragmented perception into every separate thing or being you perceive, when truly all that exists is One Love.

This negative state of mind, that some people call the ego, is only a thought but because this part of mind uses the power of the One Mind it feels powerful indeed.

It feels as if it could control and tread upon all that you hold dear. It feels as if it grabs your mind and drags you into dark and fearful places. But what actually is this so called negative power? It is a thought, built up over millennia of worldly time until it feels tangible and inescapable. This is not so!

Where is a thought when you do not think it?

It has no existence.

**When you do not think fear, guilt or loss,
Love shines through!**

Love is the only true power and all else a fearful illusion. Full authority is given to all in equal measure. This authority may be used in an instant by remembering that Love is the only true power and what you are, is Love.

Your experience of the world is determined by your choice to follow ego fear thoughts or to expand into Love existence. Every generation has known there is a choice to follow Love or turn away from Love. When one has turned away from Love repeatedly it feels as if there is no way back. But there is a very simple way back.

There are many levels of consciousness that you have access to while you wander in your thoughts. There are subconscious thoughts, conscious thoughts, higher conscious thoughts, super consciousness and many levels in between.

But know this; there are only ever two thought processes: Love or fear and only one may be chosen in any moment.

Whether you think in religious names or levels of consciousness, **anyone at any time can, with sincere intent, reach within to their Higher Consciousness and ask to be guided by Love and Truth instead of ego.**

This will feel dualistic because it feels as if you have two minds, one in negativity and one in Truth, Love and Joy. This is because negative thought has made, in your experience, a split mind. This is how life in the world is experienced.

*There is no physical entity of evil, just an accumulation of mistaken thoughts. But vigilance **is** needed to guard your thoughts from straying down a well-trodden path of fearful illusions, attack and defence.*

The concept of armour should be understood as an authority of vigilance against ego choices for fear instead of Love."

CHAPTER 2

UNEXPECTED PHYSICAL GUIDANCE

A few days later when I started my meditation, I stated that my intention was always to link into a source from Love and Light and that I only want to hear Truth, which is a statement that I make every time I ask for communication.

I was told to 'just be' and my hands were led to move, without the use of my will. My hands removed my reading glasses and were guided to follow the contours of my body, starting at my face, then neck, shoulders, chest, abdomen, hips and down to my feet. I did not move a muscle of my own volition and just trusted and allowed the beautiful movements. I was told that I had angels around me. My left hand was led out and seemed to be placed on an angel's shoulder. Then my right hand was guided out, palm upwards. In my inner vision I was given a ball of golden light from another angel and guided to place it on my abdomen. The information I received was that this light would be absorbed straight into my solar plexus where it would feed all the other energy centers of my body with Light energy.

A marvellous feeling of completeness came over me and in that moment I needed nothing, wanted nothing; no striving, no longing, just utter completeness.

I thanked the angels, then, as if in an unheard golden whisper, I was asked to go into my experience of the world and make it a Blissful experience.

I was left with a quiet wondering; how does one experience a Blissful world with all that we encounter?

One morning while washing the dishes at the sink, I went into prayer, asking sincerely that, every time I react from a negative state instead of from Love guidance, I could be made aware of this. This would then enable me to choose again and realign. I gave thanks for everything and praised the wonder of the world. Then I felt the spinning feeling in my head and the pleasant sensation of my spine lengthening. The room took on a glow even though it was cloudy outside. I knew I was connecting into an experience and I surrendered my whole will to Love Source. I was led into a beautiful sequence of movements of my whole body; stretching, turning, bending, some movements similar to tai chi, some resembling yoga and some dancelike. I was being moved by a gentle power which seemed to come from a source other than myself. **My body and my muscles were completely relaxed and I was not moving by my own decisions or impulses.**

On two occasions I was guided to lean backwards until I thought my body could not bend anymore. I was in complete surrender and trust in these guided movements. Still my body arched backwards further and further until my head was level with things on the draining board! This was not a movement I could have done then or since by using my own strength or flexibility!

When this thorough workout ended, I stood in a marvellous state of Peace that seemed limitless, as if nothing in the whole world could throw me off balance. Filled with astonishment and curiosity about what had just happened, I knew there must be a reason and I simply trusted. Restarting the washing–up, with what must have been a puzzled look on my face, I chuckled now and then at the comical nature of it. A perplexed smile stayed on my face all day as I mused at how I had been flexed in a way I could not have achieved myself, and been inspired into beautiful movements that I had never experienced before.

Was I being tested to see if I would bend over backwards for my desire to hear Truth? Was I being flexed in order to free me from a rigid way of being, or even to enable a release of stagnant and limiting thought patterns?

Alice: "I have a few questions relating to my nursing and therapeutic work. Please would you tell me about pharmaceutical drugs?"

Higher Consciousness: "From a place of Highest Pure Love, drugs are seen as ego bound, full of fear and can produce much pain and suffering themselves. They give very illusionary effects within the illusionary world. These effects are expected by the makers all along the line; right from the designers of these substances to the packers, to the distributors to the takers. They are not designed just to heal, but to fill the gaps in the perceived world of need i.e. money. This is why drugs only go a certain way along the path to help the illusion of pain and suffering because they are not based entirely on Love but on ego. However, on the ego level that most people are experiencing, drugs can be helpful because they work at the level of illusion where you think you currently abide."

Alice: "Would you tell me about Flower Essence Remedies [1] which help to balance the thought patterns?"

Higher Consciousness: "Each part of worldly creation - plant, mineral, animal, human etc - has decided on roles to carry out, parts

---

[1] Flower Essences are subtle remedies made to imbue a liquid with the beneficial healing essence of the plant.

to play in the grand scheme. The guardian angels of each form of being were there at the time these choices were made. The guardian angels still reside over these roles in all manner of ways, for example to keep the properties of metals liquid under certain circumstances and strong and rigid under others. The properties of plants were decided also. Hardly any of the properties of substances have been rediscovered by humans. I say rediscovered because you were all there when all was manifested.

One of the makers of flower remedies, Dr. Bach, opened his connectivity with the True Mind (some people would say 'listened to the Higher Consciousness') while gazing lovingly at flowers, with healing in his intentions. He encountered a tiny amount of the knowledge that is available to all. That role of flowers to help balance the mind has always been there. The guardian angels and spirit caretakers of the flowers continually make this possible.

Flowers are literally offering themselves. They are a gift; a gift of exquisite vibration of subtle form. They have many offerings, of beauty and colour, of fragrance, of healing and of nutrition. Their subtle vibration can be just the right vibration to rebalance certain mind conditions. Flowers are a very pure vibration, like spirit in form, as everything is, although most things appear to take on much more density."

Alice: "Must a person know that the flower remedies will be healing?"

Higher Consciousness: "For a person to decide to take the remedies, they have already been led to them, either by their conscious mind if they are tuned into spirit, or by their Higher Mind (whether consciously aware of it or not) which knows the flowers will be healing for them. So in answer to your question, the person will already know.

Because people have chosen to take on material form, they have a need to do material things to make a change, for example, have an operation, or take a drug or subtle plant energy. One day people will realise they do not need to do anything physical to make changes, but people's belief in physicality is too strong at present to uphold this. When that realisation occurs, there will be no need for the body or for anything material around you."

Alice: "Please would you make a comment on spiritual, or hands-on healing?"

Higher Consciousness: "Spiritual healing is when one person or groups of people ask for re-connectedness with their True Self. Some individuals will be thought of as the recipients and the others the givers, when in reality all is one. However, when more than one person asks, the request is magnified. Even if spiritual healing is carried out for oneself, this will send ripples of healing throughout all creature kind.

Spiritual healers put themselves into a place of Love to ask for this re-connectedness, and the shift is made away from an ego place. While this is happening, some healers will undoubtedly slip in and out of ego in a small or significant way during the healing. This will occur when they have thoughts of imposing healing in a certain way on the recipient. A Love-led healer will recognise this and will let those thoughts go, opening up the channels of unopposed healing which will then be received or rejected by the recipient. The ego-led healer will continue to have thoughts on 'the problem to be solved'. The Love-led healer will see beyond the perception of illness to the Perfection That Is, whilst simultaneously maintaining compassion for the other person who is experiencing the illness.

Spiritual healing is simply opening up to God energy and a bringing back of balance, without intermediate use of worldly substances or interventions. It is tapping into the realisation that you are not body but are simply God energy made of Love."

You will notice that, as I documented these words under guidance, I was led to use a capital letter for the word Love and for certain other words, being told that these words represent the principal expressions of Love.

After meditating in the garden and gazing at the wildlife, I asked:

Alice: "Am I no more important than a bird or an ant?"

Higher Consciousness: "You are no more important as you are all one in the almighty scheme but you do have a different level of conscious awareness. The ant and the bird are equally going about their daily tasks but the difference is that, in the case of these creatures, there is a degree of anonymity in being part of a huge group consciousness and thinking with the group mind.

Humans have developed an individual consciousness as well as being part of the group consciousness, although most have lost awareness of the group mind. This perception of individuality seems to make humans feel more important, but important is not the word, as the ant form and the human form are all equally illusionary."

Alice: "An acquaintance of mine is carrying long-term anger about something, which is causing her pain. How should I think of this?"

*Higher Consciousness: "See her so filled with Light and Love that there is no room for unforgiving thoughts and no desire for them. There is no painful transformation, just a gentle dissolving of them. These thoughts will bring you into a loving state of consciousness. Next, see her forgiving everyone, **even herself.** Unforgiveness is condemnation. There is no-one outside, or separate from, yourself. So who is doing the condemning and who is it being done to?*

In a dream, who are all the characters? They are all facets of one-self. This world is but a dream and unless you can forgive others you are condemning yourself to perpetual unhappiness. These subconscious thoughts need to be brought into awareness for what they are; mistaken self-condemnation projected onto another player in the dream. These mistaken thoughts can be corrected by recognising that you are not tarnished or damaged, and you have never sinned because there is no sin. There are only mistaken thoughts and these can be corrected by realising the true knowledge that all is really One mind, perfect, pure, infinite and completely made of Love."

Alice: "Oh gosh,............oh gosh." All I could do was to sit in silence.

CHAPTER 3

SUBTLE SENSATIONS

Alice: "I saw in a TV documentary, an upsetting scene of dogs in a small wire cage, all on top of each other, very scared, looking out through the wire mesh. They were to be used for food. You have said that wherever we focus our mind becomes our so called 'reality'. Does this mean that I conjured up this horrible scene with my subconscious fear thoughts?"

Higher Consciousness: "Oh Alice, thoughts are never individual. Thoughts from your lower consciousness state did this, in collaboration with the group ego. This is the same as when your altered state of consciousness can put unreal pictures into your sleeping dreams."

Alice: "But I was shocked to see it and it was completely unexpected. I had not been thinking fearful thoughts; in fact I had been quite happy before I saw that scene. How could I have constructed that?"

Higher Consciousness: "Mankind's ego consciousness is very devious and will quickly distract you out of happiness. You feel it is very powerful as it seems at times to control you. Fortunately, you have a warning whenever ego consciousness tries to take a strong hold. This warning is discomfort. You feel physical discomfort or mental discomfort. Always remember that any discomfort, anxiety, anger or fear shows you are strongly in ego. This allows you to try, if it is your desire, to come back into your Higher Consciousness and realise that reality is pure Love and Joy; all else is non-reality."

Alice: "Surely pain and discomfort are not caused by the True Mind?"

Higher Consciousness: "No. As you slip out of True Mind you slip more towards ego mind. This slip into ego, to a varying degree, is bound to be anything but joyful and the alteration of vibration activates a change of sensation. This change of sensation ideally should be used as a signal that a shift has occurred. If this signal is missed or ignored, a further shift into ego may occur, bringing increasing feelings of discomfort mentally, emotionally or physically.

If this is not realised, a whole train of events then follows, with ego giving pain which brings with it fear and anger. This pain and fear can then become manifest in the ego illusion either in your surroundings or in your body. This pain that you see or feel then generates more fear and the illusion deepens. So a useful sensation, if a shift out of Joy occurs, is often missed."

Alice: "I think I have instinctively known this deep down, but I wish someone would have actually taught me this! It is not mainstream knowledge and I expect many people are unaware of it."

Higher Consciousness: "Instinctiveness is not used by the majority of people. In your world, at this time, instinctiveness is looked upon as weird and is not respected. It is looked on as 'out of this world' and so it is! It is outside your world of ego. One knows when something is not right, but how often is that feeling ignored or belittled?

Everyone has freedom of choice and some people will go right to the depths of ego, to the brink of self-annihilation within the dream, before they listen to that chink of knowing; that chink of knowing that there is another way. Then they start their search for Truth.

Other people have strong intuitive and instinctual perception and follow it with a discerning Love-led mind which leads them to Truth and beauty. As they train themselves more in Truth and beauty, they ask for more connectedness with the Source of Truth and they do obtain it. They often do not have any organised way i.e. religion, but they just follow Love and Truth. These people have

22

searched and made a connection to their Higher Consciousness, or Right Mind. These people will know when they are out of Right Mind. The Higher Consciousness is ever present; available for the mind to become aware of it at any time, whatever state of vibration anyone is experiencing. The Higher Consciousness relies on the willingness of someone to want to connect to Love. It will not impose a higher vibration; there must be willingness to drop away from ego clutches and soar into Love and Joy, and the Love connection is right there. It was there all along. In fact you are lying comfortably in the arms of Love always, without realising it.

Just as there is a collective Love Consciousness, there is also a collective ego consciousness or thought pattern, held in the mind, which can add to the distorted perception of living in fear instead of Love. Even an innocent child may feel influenced by the group-ego, although every being has a choice about whether to be affected by something or not.

If a choice is made to follow ego thought patterns, however unaware a person is of this choice, then the ego fear-anxiety state can seem to be the normal state, and the subtle sensations of slipping out of Love are never felt. The shifts into deeper and deeper ego are felt as the pain of fear, jealousy, anger, despair. These feelings are so powerful that they seem to overcome one's True Self completely and there is a feeling of being in the clutches of this depraved state. But there is always the choice to choose differently; to see the situation from another perspective and at this point people often ask for help, for a way out. It is always there. Just a change of perception opens up the energy flows, and the pathway back to Love is revealed.

All along the path, the choice for ego state or to live in Love is available and the experience will often be of alternation between the two."

I was experiencing a dip in income and my mind kept dwelling on paying the bills and how much we have to earn just to make ends meet. But I am learning that it is important to shed negative thoughts as soon as they arise, to prevent negativity from materialising into what then becomes my experience. I kept trying to bring my mind back to Peace, but it repeatedly slipped back into ego. I tried again and asked, "Loving Oneness, Higher Consciousness, please help me. My mind has gone into petty, silly fears again." I took a big sigh, dropped my shoulders, relaxed my whole body and surrendered with Love intention.

A gentle sensation of spinning and of a spiral of energy rising within me occurred, then a feeling of becoming aligned and still. The sun beamed in through the window from the winter sky and bathed me. I relished this feeling. Joy filled me. I breathed the warmth of the sun's rays deep into my body, and in that moment something magical happened. There was no longer the sense of the sun's rays being separate from me. An overwhelming sensation filled me that the sun's rays were **one** with me and I was **one** with the sun's rays. Beauty of beauty and wonder of wonder! For a brief time I knew there was nothing at all in the whole of creation except Light. There was no me, I had no body, there was no start or end of Light, there was no start or end of anything. Everything was Pure Light, Beauty…. Peace…. Oneness.

After a few moments I became thought again. Then I began to feel the denseness of my body although I was still filled with wonder. If only I could carry this feeling of Joy and Light with me! I started to realise that in those moments of total surrender to Love Consciousness, amazing things happen.

Alice: "Christianity says that Jesus is the only way to God. I find this idea feels exclusive and seems to negate all the other paths. Please explain."

*Higher Consciousness: "Do not be tense with this question. Jesus has gone before and he bore with him the Christ energy. He is a realised soul. He realised the Oneness with all and the fact that there never was anything but Oneness. The **realisation of Oneness** is the way.*

*Jesus is more than a name. The word is synonymous with the Way, the Truth and the Life. He manifested Supreme Love in human form. This empowered people so they could, and still can, believe it possible to follow in his footsteps. Jesus was filled with The Spirit of Supreme Love, which Christians call The Holy Spirit, because he always was and **is** the Spirit of Supreme Love. You will one day be ready to accept that you, and every other being, are also completely united with the Power of this Spirit and that it is not outside you, but within.*

This truly universal power is available to all; all faiths, all religions, all manifestations, and will be named differently in different cultures.

The Christian religion is not the only way to the Highest Power of Love. The Highest Power is all-encompassing, all-loving, all-inclusive and cannot be reduced, restricted or compartmentalised. Doctrines will need to be examined if Truth and Love is to be followed, to discern the true from the false.

*Tuning in with **your** Higher Consciousness, whatever name you call it, will give full access to the totality of Supreme Love, connecting all with all. By tuning into your Higher Consciousness, with the intent of reaching deeper into Love, you will be led to the consciousness through which Jesus lived. Christians may call it The Christ Consciousness or Christ Mind but these are just Christian*

25

terms for what is a truly universal path. This waits for all who call to Supreme Love.

A heart led by Love, a spirit led by Joy, a mind led by Oneness, will always reach Supreme Love or, in words of your culture, God.

When the willingness is shown, the Universal Power opens up to you, wherever you live, whether you follow a religion or not. This power will connect your spirit-of-life to the Christ Consciousness, or whatever Holy name this path is given. Only a glimmer of willingness is needed for a miraculous chain of events to occur."

Alice: "There are so many names that I could use when communicating with you. What name should I use?"

Higher Consciousness: "When you ask a question, go to your Highest Good. It does not matter what name, as it is the intention in your heart and in your thoughts that is important. Your intention-thoughts are always vibrated and heard before any words or names."

Alice: "That is beautiful."

Higher Consciousness: "Names do have special vibrations because of the importance that has been placed upon them, but a name makes things easier for usage. Language is very necessary to communicate between people in your world, but language takes on a different meaning in Heaven. Words as such are not necessary because the vibration of the intention is enough. In Heaven everything is instant; the intention is simultaneous with the movement of energy, and the only energy is Love.

For simplicity I will use terms that are easily understood in your culture, but dearest child, in your mind, keep things universal. Do not pigeon-hole God into one language, or one culture."

Alice: "Pure Spirit of Love, if I want to reach towards the Highest Love, what sort of image could I have in my mind when wanting to connect?"

Higher Consciousness: "To imagine the most beautiful colour, the most wonderful aroma, the most angelic music, the most amazing sunset, the most loving embrace, or the most beautiful creature, could not reach the beauty of the True Consciousness. So just be. Gently empty the mind. Stop all images. Do not try for anything. Gently surrender with the intention of Love filling you."

My husband and I have been concerned for the health and attitudes of someone close to us. We are trying to help them but feel as if the help is not being accepted. I prayed and asked if I should approach this person to offer to do healing work with them.

Higher Consciousness: "They are not willing to be receptive to that approach at the moment, but hold them in your mind lovingly and clearly visualise every tool or implement they use in their work radiating wonderful Light to them. Imagine this Light is Love and it is absorbed willingly into their very being. Imagine clearly, every morsel of food or drop of liquid that they consume being filled with Light and Love and this Light seeping into their every cell. Imagine clearly, the ground they walk on being made of Light and Love and this Light being absorbed through their feet and travelling up their body. See them filled with Light; this Light being Love and Joy."

I started doing this a few times a day. It was a wonderful experience to see Light emanating from everything and being absorbed by this person willingly in my visualisation of them, and bringing wonderment to them.

Alice: "Higher Consciousness, what is the primary thing I need to work on in my life?" I went into the quiet and waited. My hands were led out to my sides, then up into prayer position.

Higher Consciousness: "Presence of mind." was the reply.

I was puzzled at first, and then understood. If my mind is present, if I am in the present moment and in my True Spiritual Mind, not my bodily ego mind, then everything else flows in a loving way. If I am thinking worldly thoughts, ego troubled thoughts, a variety of trials and tribulations will come about.

Alice: "How can I be in my spiritual right mind any more than I am trying to be at present?"

Higher Consciousness: "Come into your loving mind as frequently as you remember. State your intention to be guided by your Higher Mind. Pray or meditate every morning. Even on busy days a few seconds of intention can be fitted in. Keep remembering to be present with The Higher Consciousness in all your tasks."

Alice: "How can I keep my mind on a Higher Consciousness and carry out busy tasks? Will I not have accidents and make mistakes if my mind is not on the task?"

*Higher Consciousness: "The half-way house to True Awakening is living the Love-led state **in the world**. When you are thinking Love almost all the time, life and tasks run smoothly and harmoniously, with challenges easily handled. Do not forget, whatever you project into your world, from your state of mind, becomes what appears to be your 'reality'."*

Alice: "I think I need the true definition of Love. I can see that the Love of which you speak is not romantic love or love of possessions, lifestyles, circumstances or even an emotional reaction to a person or event."

Higher Consciousness:

*"**Love is a power**,*

A power that can move all things.

Love is the only power and could be called the Universal Energy.

Love is the pure abundance of Light, so all-encompassing that nothing else exists.

Love is completeness. Nothing else is needed or will ever be needed.

Love is Oneness everlasting,

Love is beauty, Love is Joy,

Love is God and God is Love."

CHAPTER 4

DEFENCE AND ATTACK

Alice: "I know this might sound laughable, but please would you tell me how to grow vegetables without them all being eaten by slugs! It is my desire not to kill anything but my vegetable plot has been decimated!"

Higher Consciousness: "As all of creation gradually strives towards the Light, various levels of consciousness will be attained, culminating in a loving, harmonious state but still within the dream, before final awakening to Perfect Oneness.

In this harmonious state, everything lives in Peace and accord. Eventually no food is required except for nourishment in pure energy form, with no predator or prey and no need to kill."

Alice: "If food is in endless supply, would not the population of everything explode?"

Higher Consciousness: "With everything living in harmony there is no fear and therefore no base instinct to repeatedly procreate to protect the species. Numbers of creatures are therefore in harmony.

You are living in a state of illusion which does not yet resemble a harmonious state. Your dream still includes nightmare scenes played out before you and in your imaginings. This includes your vegetables and fruits being consumed and destroyed by slime-covered creeping things which lurk under every stone and crevice. While you seem to be in this nightmare, you will also seem to need to react in defence and attack.

One day, and it can be in this lifetime, you and multitudes of others will change your mind, literally, and realise all this is a dream, conjured by the imaginings of an insane mind.

31

The Highest Love would not create such a world as this, which includes much suffering and pain.

One day you will all change the group-mind and find yourselves more and more in harmony and on the homecoming back to Peace.

*Insects and other creatures can only live in harmony with you if you truly believe they can, but at the moment you still believe they can cause harm. Until your **belief** system changes, you will need to act appropriately according to how you are perceiving.*

You cannot change what appears to be your physical universe without changing your belief system.

When you realise that your thoughts create what you see, you may lay down your arms and gradually start to see things differently.

But hear this, you will not be able to see things differently from the ego mind patterns, as they are the mind patterns which brought you here and which try to keep you besieged.

*While you seem to be giving your power to living in the ego state, instead of living in Love and acceptance, it feels as if you have lost your power and are weak. This perpetuates the fear/attack state. You are ignoring and disregarding your power while you stumble in this worldly dream, but you can 're-cognise' your power; literally re-think it, address it and embrace it by choosing to go to **your Higher Consciousness** and asking to see situations **from that higher state**. Every time you do this you are helping the **whole of creation** as everyone is completely linked, with no separation.*

Living in a harmonious state includes having virtually no fear. When absolutely no fear is experienced, there will no longer be a need for physicality, as physicality is an illusion of fear, experienced by the collective ego mind and the only reality is Spirit. The collective ego mind has fabricated a world of suffering and fear, with one life-form against another. When there is no fear, a formless state of existence of sheer bliss is experienced within total Love."

Alice: "So let me try to understand this. The fact that I am seeing attack anywhere, (not just relating to slugs!) shows that I am led by the negative ego part of my mind which believes in fear, defence and attack. It is not until I let go of these beliefs that I will experience any lasting harmony.

I cannot let go of these beliefs from my ego consciousness. I must go to my Higher Consciousness and have the firm intent to experience from Love instead of fear and surrender into this. From this place of surrender, my belief in a fearful world will gradually reduce. This will increase my belief in a harmonious world which will more and more become the reality.

Phew! I am going to need **much** more help with this."

Higher Consciousness: "There are many teachers and books of wisdom, truth and Love to help unpeel false beliefs. Did you think it was a coincidence when that book 'A Course in Miracles' fell off that market stall into your hands 10 years ago; the book you have never opened all these years and always meant to open? Do you think it is coincidence that you are noticing that book on the shelf more lately?

*Realisation can come in an instant or can be slow and progressive; but for everyone, realisation **will** come. Many have self-realised without any external tool.*

Just to go within and listen to the still small voice of Love is the route. To tune in to this voice of Truth and Love more and more and always at any sign of upset, worry or fear, you will reach the pathway of Love. Tune in and say, "I want to see this differently. I want to feel this from Love instead of fear." And at that moment open yourself to Love possibilities which are endless.

Every time you do this, the world will seem a little lighter, more loving, more harmonious. Simple loving solutions will arise in the mind when you did not think any resolution was possible.

A world of bliss will be ever nearer.

Alice: *"Sorry to get back to practicalities, but how do I deal with the slugs right now?*

Higher Consciousness: *"In practical terms, you will need to deal with slugs from the level of belief you currently hold. **Your perception of being attacked is a useful measure of your belief in the need for attack and defence.***

You have a choice; while living a nightmare, you can react with nightmare actions, with defence and attack, but this will feed the nightmare and perpetuate it. On another level, you can grow many extra crops to allow enough for all. On another level, you can work on unpeeling your false underlying beliefs. Then you will be free. Free to just be. Free to just love, and free to live life like a gentle in-breath and out-breath in balanced harmony."

Alice: "Higher Consciousness, I do not feel as if I am progressing spiritually. I slip and fall back so easily and go into little ego concerns such as, whether I am performing well enough at work etc and I slip into little defensive thoughts, even though I know intellectually that there is nothing to fear."

Higher Consciousness: "Alice, you are progressing with your willingness. Willingness to reach Love and become Love is the biggest necessity to reaching that pure state. You say you do not feel any difference but you are changing. Do you not feel negative feelings, when they arise, as more painful to your being?"

Alice: "Yes I do, and little upsets feel like big painful issues."

Higher Consciousness: "This is because you are listening to the shifts in consciousness more. When you shift into a fear/ego state you feel the change more acutely. This is good because it is a clear reminder to you that you have slipped out of your True Consciousness, and you then have the choice to bring yourself back to a Love-led state.

This is exactly the same as in the case of illness symptoms. They are reminders that someone has ignored the first signs of unease. They have not corrected themselves and thought through their feelings from a place of Love instead of fear. The fear has swept them along until the fear state seems the 'normal state'. Abundance of compassion is needed, as people can feel as if they are totally trapped in this state. The negative/fear state, if not corrected, ultimately ends up in illness for the ego. Do not forget, any negative feeling, anger, hurt, frustration, injustice, abandonment, greed, lack, unworthiness, is based on fear and can be corrected by a willingness and a desire to see these issues through Love's eyes instead.

You, and everyone who wants to progress spiritually, will need to spend time on this and make it a priority in life. Speak to your Highest True Consciousness; ask for your perception of an issue to be changed to a Love perception and wait in expectation and surrender.

A new perspective will be received.

A lift in comfort will be felt, even if only for a few seconds. This is a huge step. If the comfort feeling is fleeting, know that it can be increased and maintained for longer periods, but practice is needed.

If the comfort feeling lasts two seconds, and the discomfort emotion returns, then immediately reconnect with True Consciousness by asking again to see things through Love, and wait. Keep repeating this process. Eventually the Love-ease feeling will be maintained for longer and longer periods.

*Do it every day and whenever you feel without a sense of Joy and ease, and many times a day if you are in physical or mental pain. When you have asked, **surrender** to Love and wait. Do not 'will' this or that to happen; just surrender. When in an ego state of unease, you do not know what the most loving outcome should be, so just by asking to be brought back to seeing through Love's eyes, the clouds will start to lift.*

One thing you will notice when you return to true perception is that you will start to see other people as beautiful children of Light. You will see that the upsetting things that they do are just childish mistakes and desperate calls for Love. You will see that attacks are their fearful forms of defence. You will see that their grasping for possessions or power comes from a terrible fear of lack which, in reality, can only be quenched by Love. You will start to see that there is no sin and there are no sinners."

Alice: "Oh, Higher Consciousness, please could I interrupt? I have many questions. What about mass murderers and instigators of cruel genocide?"

Higher Consciousness: "Please do not forget, anything not of Love does not exist. To the ego this will seem a terrible and unacceptable statement, and may bring up much anger and resistance. To the ego, atrocities are very real. While embodied in the ego dream, worldly beings will feel the need to react from ego, according to the circumstances, until they peel back more layers of fear, and a happier world will manifest.

Mass murder is the culmination of fears from a mass consciousness, brought into the dream which is your world. It is the imagined materialisation of your biggest, most terrible fears. It is fear of hell being played out in your dream because you empower what you dwell on in your thoughts, just as in your sleeping dreams.

Just to know this can give hope; hope that everyone can, inch by inch, lift themselves out of ego negativity into a happier dream-state, to ultimately what can be a blissful world while still on Earth. This can be done in an instant but usually realisation takes patience, much practice and devotion.

Even if someone is in a terrible place of hurt and upset, having lost a loved one in unutterable circumstances, it is possible to ask to see this differently and little chinks of light will open up when there only seemed hell before. If this exercise is repeated and repeated, those chinks of light will grow and the pain in the heart will ease.

The world around will seem to change with the desire to see the world differently. People will seem more loving. Colours will seem brighter. The occurrence of negative happenings will decrease, and there will gradually be more awareness when a negative attitude is being held instead of a Loving one, giving the chance to choose again. The blissful state will be nearer. The blissful state can be lived."

CHAPTER **5**

OBSTACLES

Alice: "Higher Consciousness, I long to create sculptures and I long to spend time in prayer and meditation, but I encounter constant obstacles. Please help me."

*Higher Consciousness: "Alice, you will not avoid obstacles while immersed in the world. The way you perceive the world **is** an obstacle to Truth. The state of consciousness, and the thoughts within this state, has made your world and all that is in it, in order to distract from the True State of Oneness. Therefore you will not escape obstacles while in the present level of consciousness and carrying your present beliefs.*

Your way of thinking got you here. Now it is time for new thinking. The time is ripe. The empowerment of choices will soon become clear."

Alice: "But how can I be creating one obstacle after another, when I am dedicating my life to finding Truth?"

*Higher Consciousness: "You would not be making obstacles to Truth unless part of you was fearful **of** Truth. The fact that you appear to be of this world means that part of your mind is ruled by negative ego thoughts. These always nurture fear and will always conjure up obstacles. Your fearful thoughts **are fearful of you reaching your power; fearful of the totality of consciousness reaching its power and being its True Power."***

Alice: "So what can I do about this? Anyway I am not actually aware of any fear most of the time."

Higher Consciousness: "The fear we talk of is an underlying fear; deep in the subconscious, unavailable to the conscious mind. It is the driving force of all ego thoughts and is the main instigator of the

39

mistaken, but deeply held, core belief. It is, at its root, a fear for survival and of complete annihilation, which lies beneath every ego thought in the huge group ego-consciousness.

Whenever you feel able, watch your thoughts and remember to ask yourself, *"Where does that thought come from; what is driving it? What is deep down beneath it?"* Behind many, many thoughts are **the debased and distorted thoughts of the ego, driving mankind from thoughts of Truth, to dwell on misperceptions of unworthiness.** These then become carried as a burden throughout your experiences.

But hear this, my child, every being is exquisitely loved and is completely worthy of the Joy which is your birthright. There is nothing that anyone has ever done or will ever do, that can remove or reduce this. This is inherent in all of creation and waits for you to merely ask for it.

As the obstacles you perceive are caused by this unconscious fear, let go of more and more fear every day.

Go to your Peace.

Changes can only be made from within.

The whole world can be changed from within and this is the only way

change can occur.

Feel your inner Light; your inner Love.

Know that your Love is everyone's Love.

There is no separation.

Feel the power of the Infinite Love Consciousness.

There is only Oneness.

This power is Supreme.

There are no obstacles to this.

But ego illusion tells you there are.

What is ego? It is a negative fear-based thought.

Does a thought have a substance? No.

Does a negative thought have power? No.

Does it have existence? No.

*Then visualise ego leaving your body and mind and disintegrating into the **nothingness** that it is. Do not see it stored or pushed away; visualise that it has completely gone and has no existence.*

See, in your mind's eye, that Power, Love and Light has no opposite and know that this is your natural state. Fear has no power over you.

Every day, say this and do this and carry less and less of the unacknowledged and previously unaddressed fear that underlies all.

Let your True Self shine through.

Be determined now. This is what you want."

Alice: "Thank you, thank you."

So I began to understand, but not yet able to fully believe, that an experience that befalls us only does so to the extent of our belief in it, and the permission we have subconsciously given for our participation.

Alice: "So this will gradually deal with the underlying fear that causes obstacles, but how should I handle obstacles when they occur?"

Higher Consciousness: "We are glad you have asked this question today. From the level of consciousness that you are experiencing, you feel that creating sculpture is important to your happiness. Everyone has wants and desires that they think will bring happiness. Then fears of not achieving your goals will be conjured up and of course your experience will always reflect these fears by creating obstacles.

As for dealing with obstacles as they occur, deal with them lovingly, without hurry or grievance. Put no importance on your personal goals which you perceive as so significant. Every time anyone reacts lovingly, in any situation, the consciousness of the whole planet is raised, as all is One.

Go to your Peace and ask your Higher Consciousness to help you see perfection everywhere and Love shining in everything. Carry less fear of non-achieving every day. Less fear will lessen the occurrence of what you perceive as obstacles and will open up a clear pathway for whatever makes you happy!"

Alice: "That is beautiful, thank you, but that is a tall order, which I may never achieve. Oops! There I go again!"

I sat quietly, mulling over what I had received. Feeling such gratitude, I asked, "How can I thank you?"

Higher Consciousness: "When you are holding your child lovingly in your arms, do you need them to thank you? No, all you want to do is love them."

Alice: "Would you say more about a blissful world?"

Higher Consciousness: "A blissful world begets a life of purity, free from layers of guilt, attachment, loss, greed, anger or fear. Imagine all of life and all creation only echoing Love to one another! Life calls out with a resounding, "Yes!" with fun, laughter and singing. Colours will be resonating all around with the different aspects of Love, Peace, Joy, sharing, celebrating, serenity, Oneness.

A blissful world is a state of being wherein there is a knowing that all is linked; supremely One, with no separation, and that giving does not mean a loss of anything, but always a gain."

One morning I entered the kitchen and discovered the antique breadboard, which could be damaged by immersing in water, had been used for cutting meat again by family and now needed to be washed. I became irritated because I have asked on many occasions for this not to happen. I had been in a state of Peace and harmony, and to become upset by something so petty seemed ridiculous and I felt as if I had failed again. "Please help me."

Higher Consciousness: "Dear Alice, learning and re-aligning is an ongoing process, not an instant event. Challenges will present themselves and the ego thought patterns will try to take you out of your Peace no matter how minor the challenge.

Be assured, you can see these as gifts to you. They are opportunities to realise, more and more, that ego thoughts can be changed into Loving thoughts just by observing them and choosing again.

*When you became angry, you were not angry about the breadboard, but upset because your requests had been disregarded, therefore you felt **you** had been disregarded and disrespected. Your ego thoughts made very full use of this and immediately jumped, in telling you that you do not deserve any respect as you are worthless and therefore at risk of harm or even annihilation. This is how everyone's ego works, bringing fear into the simplest of situations. The ego part of everyone's mind is highly alert and vigilant about using any and every possibility to bring anxiety and fear. Your ego also immediately told you to put up a defence to this, and the ego's best defence is always attack. The ego's thoughts are always based on separation, 'them against me', but the Truth is total Oneness and only Love.*

Knowing this, you can bring yourself back into the present moment, instead of allowing thoughts to rush off into future or past distressing scenarios, and choose again. You can choose Truth. The Truth is that you do deserve respect, you are all worthy and you are all perfect creations held in perfect Oneness."

I began to start watching my thoughts and where they were taking me, and smiling, almost laughing, at the tricks my ego mind was playing.

While working in my living room one day, dusting ornaments in a mindful way, I chanced to ask, "How can I ever reach enlightenment?" I paused and waited.

I received an unexpected response. "I am the Enlightenment Angel. I have a role which was given to me. I am that role, of progressing the enlightenment on Earth. I do not deviate from that role and have no desire or capacity to stray from that role. I am very powerful but will never use my influence until people have the desire to reach towards the Light. When people have sincere desire to feel Love and express Love, this opens up all possibilities to reach Oneness."

Alice: "Where are you?"

Angel: "I am in your mind but not of your mind. I am an individual within the Oneness."

Alice: "Is there just one of you?"

Angel: "There is just one of me but I am not limited in time and space. My intention allows multidimensional possibilities. Happenings instigated by me are quantum. The tiniest glimmer of desire to 'be the Love you are' puts into place more opportunities than you would ever imagine. Most opportunities are not seen, not heard, or are rejected, as Love thoughts are swiftly followed by negative doubt. If people could laugh at doubt, a momentum towards Love-Existence would ensue of momentous proportions."

Alice: "Going on the idea that we make our own life experiences depending on whether we are led by Love or led by fear, I have this question. If a puppy only sees the world as a fun, lovely place to explore, and everyone as a friend, why might another dog snap at it, if the pup ran over to say hello? Surely negativity would not even be in its consciousness and, as we make our own 'reality', could an innocent pup create a negative situation?"

*Higher Consciousness: "Ego consciousness is handed down through generations and the ego illusion enters at conception. Otherwise, why would human babies cry and have fears of neglect and non-survival. Fear of survival is also held strongly in the group-unconscious mind, completely generated by the mass-ego thoughts. This influences expectations subconsciously and therefore influences perceived experiences. Do not forget, this whole worldly experience is an illusion. Therefore, if someone perceives an attack, it is a projection of **their** ego thoughts combined with the mass-ego thoughts which fabricates their experience."*

Alice: "Higher Love, I do not seem to have my usual deep contented happiness and there does not seem to be any reason. Everything is going well, just busy. What is going on?"

Higher Consciousness: "You have not consciously reconnected with Source, or even with your desire to do so, for some time due to being busy and tired. Love Source is always with you and throughout you, but at these times you are not so aware of the Joy and the Love that is all around. When you do not positively link with Love, ego negativity will swiftly grasp your thought patterns and sweep you as far into loveless thoughts as you will allow."

I sat and asked to be connected deeply with the Higher Consciousness, and totally surrendered. Oh, wonder of wonder. Just by finding five minutes to do this, I suddenly felt so different, so lifted. But I realised I was probably harbouring things under the surface in my subconscious and, if that were the case, I wanted to bring any negativity or false beliefs to the surface to deal with them, to clear them from deep down.

I embarked on an experiment. Because I am trained as a Homeopath, I mentally prepared myself and took a specialised homeopathic remedy to unblock suppressed emotions, warning my husband in case of a few unsettled days! Within 24 hours I experienced an outpouring of pent-up anger, sadness and grief, the depth and breadth of which I had not known I was carrying. Making time to address this I sat at the bottom of the garden alone, knowing I could hand this all over to a higher level of my consciousness to be cleared lovingly. After meditating for a while I asked to connect with Love Consciousness, and asked what on Earth all the hidden anger and sadness was about, as I am a very happy, positive person.

Stating that I would like to release any negativity, I surrendered to Supreme Love. The response I received was a gentle reminder of the explanation of the innocent puppy scenario, that everyone in this worldly illusion can unconsciously choose to be influenced to some degree by the collective ego, and I was told:

Higher Consciousness: "Over the years, consciously and subconsciously, everyone who 'forgets' to see past the illusion will feel as if they accumulate negative memory. This would be intolerable for the conscious mind. Therefore, what seems like linear negative memories are suppressed into the subconscious, to emerge from time to time and covertly influence automatic reactions."

Alice: "So this is a marvellous opportunity to shed some of this from my subconscious. I am ready to be rid of these uncomfortable emotions. Please show me how."

Higher Consciousness: "You can simply state your intention from a place of sincerity while reaching to a Higher Love state, or you could use a powerful visualisation. For example, visualise this negativity as little black parcels, boxes and shapes emerging from you and let them go. In your mind, give them to me."

Alice: "I visualised many of them; spiky ones and sludgy ones. They all faded and disappeared as soon as I handed them over to Higher Consciousness."

Higher Consciousness: "They have gone to the nothing that they were. They never had any real power, you just thought they had."

Alice: "Higher Consciousness, now that I understand, could I do it again?"

Higher Consciousness: "Yes, go ahead."

I went within and visualised again.

Alice: "I cannot even see black packages this time, just a few grey shapes." I willingly handed these over to Love Consciousness, and felt them melt to nothing. "Please could I be filled with Joy instead?" I surrendered again to enable this to happen. Instantly, the angry, upset feelings were gone. I felt calmer, lighter and at ease with the world, as if a weight had been lifted from me. "Thank you, Higher Consciousness. I must try to remember to hand those feelings over whenever I am aware of them because I know there will be a next time and a next time."

Of course I would not have taken the powerful unsuppressing remedy to delve into the dark recesses of my mind if I had not been totally confident of handing it all over to the powerful Consciousness of Love.

"What should I do now?"

Higher Consciousness: *"Just sit for a moment and visualise Love and Joy filling your heart area. See it as a beautiful light. See the Light filling your whole chest, your arms and hands, your neck and head, your whole torso, legs and feet. See and feel it surrounding you. Marvel and revel in it! It is meant to give supreme pleasure!"*

Alice: "Oh wonderful! I feel so lifted **so** very different from how I was a few minutes ago! Thank you."

What I did was unusual, trying to unlock things of which I was unaware, from my subconscious. It was a useful experiment, but not generally recommended or needed.

"Would it be useful for people if they simply do the handing-over visualisation whenever they are aware of not being at Peace?"

Higher Consciousness: *"Yes, if people are ready to be open to this, with an open mind, an open heart and without fear. Fear is powerless anyway. But some people are not willing to really let go of deceptions, grievances and anger and they keep these close to them, even guarding them from ever diminishing.*

In fact, handing over loveless thoughts to the Highest Love is the only way to give them up, and cannot be done through willpower or the ego mindset that put them there. You are right, homeopathy is not necessary for this and any feeling of unease may be simply handed over to the Higher Consciousness. This will reduce the Earth time spent on reaching enlightenment for all, not just that individual, and will empower a life filled with Joy. When the weights are lifted from the shoulders, the Child of Creation will soar. There will be lightness of step and a song in the heart!"

CHAPTER 6

HE WALKED BESIDE ME

While embarking on employment changes, I was feeling some stress. I tuned into Love and asked for assistance. I did not write this at the time of receiving it as I usually do, and you may see why as you read, therefore this is from my recall a few minutes later.

I was reminded that our mind is part of the One Mind, therefore our mind has huge strength. I was told that this gives us the capability to pour Grace into every circumstance, even if we perceive it as a worrying situation. I was told that it is the realisation that this is so, and the belief in it, that opens up the power. But I know it is just this realisation that I, and probably most of the world, cannot grasp.

Remembering what I had been told, I knew that if we dwell on negativity then we will perceive negative situations happening to us and around us. I knew I wanted to see the world with Grace instead of fear. Taking myself on an inward journey, I asked with sincerity and yearning, and tears in my eyes, "Please help me to be more aware of slipping into ego whenever it happens. Please take me deeper, take me closer to Love Guidance. I want to really *know* Higher Consciousness."

I went willingly and easily into a very peaceful state and waited, totally surrendering to Highest Love.

Higher Consciousness: *"Are you willing to come even closer to True Consciousness?"*

I knew that the sheer awe of approaching The Supreme Power of All would make me hold back. I surprised myself and asked for help from Jesus. It surprised me because I still feel reserved about doing anything that I deem to be 'religious'.

Deep within me I said, "Yes, I want to go closer. I want to go deeper."

I slipped into a profound, trance-like state, deeper than I had experienced before and lost awareness of space and time. Immediately I was given a crystal clear vision.

I saw Jesus holding my hand, slowly walking with me. He was looking lovingly at me, making my heart soar and enveloping me in unexplainable Love. My heart felt open and outside my body, radiating Joy to every thing. As we walked, in this super-real vision, dark shapes of all sizes swirled towards me as if they were going to hit me. Large dark blocks with sharp edges, big enough to kill me, flew through the air at me in a fierce storm. I said, "Protect me Jesus," but realised I was already protected. None of these things hit me or even touched me. Jesus said without words, *"It is just your ego mind trying to prevent you opening to Love. You can release these thoughts using my authority over them and, yes indeed, your authority which is your birthright. These flying shapes do not exist."*

One large box-shaped object flew straight at me and, with renewed assurance, I gestured to brush it aside, but even as I thought of this, it fell to the ground and turned to silver. I noticed the road we were on was silver, soft and malleable, almost molten.

We approached what I can only describe as a tabernacle, and could hear music and activity. Jesus opened a beautiful fine veil at the entrance. At this moment I wished to enter, but to be in the presence of Pure Love made me hold back. My strong desire to seek Truth gave me courage and I took a tentative step to enter into the presence of Love. Immediately my actual physical body began to quiver and twitch, and a feeling of protest, fight and struggle started as if something was trying to prevent me approaching Pure Love. I knew it was my ego thoughts and, although it was very physical, knew it actually had no power over me. I remembered being told that the ego tries to trick us, but it is only composed of misplaced thoughts built up over millennia. I asked myself, "Where is a thought when we do not think it? It has no existence." Realising this enabled me to regain my equilibrium and maintain my integrity. "You have no power over me!" I said in my mind, "You do not exist!" The twitching and the struggle stopped and my body became calm and strong.

We entered the golden light. I was so overwhelmed by what I was experiencing that I hesitated by the entrance, unable to move. I could not comprehend what I was witnessing; the entire scene being emblazoned in Light, and filled with all-encompassing Glory, worship and Love, but most of all Joy. Jesus encouraged me to step forward but, as I took one tiny step, I was overwhelmed with awe by the emanations of grandeur, and I went down onto the ground with my head on the floor. I know I was surrounded by Pure Love beings, tending and bathing me in their Glory, sweeping their golden garments around me to give nurture. These beings did not walk on the floor, but glided and swirled, their garments in motion. I stayed folded down on the floor for some time, then I was gently back in my room at home, filled with Peace, Joy, awe and wonderment.

Giving thanks with tears in my eyes and emotion welling in my throat, I was staggered by the vivid clarity and tangibility of what had happened. I gave thanks for such an experience, thanks for the courage to begin approaching The Supreme of All after searching and longing, but resisting, every day for over 30 years. Thanks also for knowing that we all have authority over negative thoughts and feelings to which we unknowingly have given the illusion of power.

We have authority to **know** that negative thoughts have **no** power, only the strength that we invest in them; authority to choose to withdraw that strength and to know that, indeed, ego has no actual existence.

Alice: "Please, Higher Love, tell me why did I have physical feelings of struggle while I was experiencing a vision with Jesus?"

Higher Consciousness: "You have given meaning to sad thoughts, destruction and death from world events and from your hospital work particularly, over many years. Because you nurtured these thoughts, it was as if they had strength. You are now realising that they have no strength in themselves. You must also know that consciousness is always group-consciousness, therefore, within the vision, you used your True Authority over negative thoughts from people who seem other than you, from times that seem other than these, from memories that were thought to hold power. These were held in thought form only; the ego thought form. The ego appears to be very powerful but it cannot create, it can only fabricate illusions. As you desired to come closer to Pure Love, these ego thoughts wanted to reinstate themselves as dominant, and show you what power they can appear to have in your subconscious. By bringing your subconscious into your consciousness, a struggle took place. This experience was from the ego mind. It conjured an illusion of negativity being an embodied strength, capable of bringing fear.

Because you had no fear, and would not interact in a way subordinate to these thoughts, your True Authority ripened and bore fruit."

Alice: "How can I maintain this positive state not just in my meditations but in day to day life? The busyness of life seems to always bring up small negativities."

Higher Consciousness: "Have the desire to live life through your Higher Consciousness. Meditate and pray every day and if possible many times per day. This way you will reinforce the higher state in your very being. "

Alice: "Are there any other requirements for reaching a more Love-Guided Consciousness?"

54

Higher Consciousness: "*The desire to reach Oneness, the Totality of Love, in other words Pure Consciousness, is the most important thing. With this comes a desire to radiate Love. These two things alone are really all that is required. By having these desires, you will be united with Love Forces which will appear to reunite you with the Bliss and beauty that you never really left.*"

Alice: "But on a worldly, practical level, is there anything we could do to help us in this process; preparation, prayers, rituals?"

Higher Consciousness: "*Keep a clean, uncluttered house and a clean, uncluttered mind. Keep a clean body whenever possible. Treat these times of connection with Higher Love as priority and not as an extra to be fitted in if the opportunity arises. In the mind desirous of obtaining and attaining the Love State, time for connection to Higher Consciousness is as important as food, water, clean air, good sleep and exercise.*

When you come to reconnect with your Spiritual True Self, quieten the mind and body. Do not completely still the mind, blocking all thoughts, but request that only thoughts of Love Source, from the Highest Good come to you. Your mind must not be blocked, but open and tuned in to Love. Just as your heart must be willing and desirous to be open to give and receive Love, not bound and rigid. Your lungs should be soft and open to the flow in and out of pure air and you could visualise that this air contains Love essence which imbues you with Peace, Joy and beauty.

Your limbs should be soft and comfortable and ready to move if the Love Stream washes them into movement. Your belly should be held softly and allowed to expand and withdraw naturally with the rise and fall of the diaphragm.

Your eyes should be soft and eyelids only closed lightly like the closing of butterfly wings. If open, the eyes should gaze gently, seeing but not seeing the material world; seeing beyond the material and seeing the gentle Consciousness of Love in everything."

Alice: "Would you tell me, what is the significance of the hands put together in prayer?"

Higher Consciousness: *"The hands are significant due to the fact that the energy of life flows freely from the palms and fingers. Placing the hands together may give the impression of the energy flow being more contained and circulating around the body. This helps the individual to feel the presence of this energy more acutely.*

Being aware of this Love Energy, that everyone has flowing through them at all times, gives a feeling of wellness and lifts the spirits. This allows the person to regain their integrity, the Peace of equilibrium, and their birthright of cohesion with all. Therefore the placing together of the hands gives a feel-good sensation which takes away tension and can help the ease of slipping into a higher state of consciousness which is even more in tune with Love. This is just one method, but ultimately no methodology is required, just the simplicity of loving thought leading to no thought, within the pure Oneness."

I very casually, without much thought, asked a question that I had previously become too tense and anxious about because it seemed so important, and which had previously made me lose communication. This time I just came out with it. "Who am I speaking to?"

Higher Consciousness: "Yourself. Your own consciousness on a higher level. The Higher Group Mind which has unrestricted links with The True Mind."

Alice: "Me !?" My thoughts raced around me and put me in a whirl. "Myself? These answers are coming from myself?? But, but...."

"Will I only hear truth?"

Higher Consciousness: "That depends on your receptivity and desire to listen to only Truth. Your desire is very deep."

Alice: "If God is the source of all I see, how could I see atrocities?"

Higher Consciousness: "God is the source of all you truly see. Seeing is different to perceiving. When you think you see atrocities, you are perceiving the experience of an illusion that is not of God, so in the deepest reality, it does not exist. I know this is very hard to comprehend as all the world around you seems and feels so real and solid. Do not forget, even the scientific world is discovering that everything is really energy in form.

You live 90% in ego dominance and some people even more, and that is the journey you are on. Ego perceptions will seem so real; forgive yourself for this. Even a small awareness of the Truth is a wonderful step towards enlightenment.

*I am teaching you, day by day that every time you have an uncomfortable feeling of fear, upset, irritation or similar, to realise that you are thinking ego thoughts from the part of your mind that has wandered away from Truth. I am reminding you to use these feelings as a tool to allow you the awareness of when you are in ego and then you may ask to see and feel through Truth instead. When you go to your Higher Consciousness and state your intention, a different perspective **will** be given.*

This journey you are on is a journey of choice. Humankind does not realise the immensity of the power of choice. Most of the day you are choosing relatively benign ego thoughts, but they are still from ego. It is only when you are challenged that your ego state rises into your awareness and then you can choose; to follow the path of suffering or to see through Love's eyes. So actually, uncomfortable feelings can be used positively.

The images of atrocities are fears that you, and people around you, carry and subconsciously manifest to play out before your bodily eyes.

Just as you realised that the dark things flying at you, and the 'physical battle' that you experienced in your body, could be recognised for what they were (conjured up illusions), so the way atrocities are experienced can be treated likewise. This is not denial or suppression. This is facing your images, not shying away from them, but realising they are images in an ego dream. You can perceive the material world but see through it to the gentle Consciousness of Love behind all images."

Alice: "Higher Consciousness, I am struggling with this concept. It is all very well seeing images flying at me in a meditative state and realising that they are nothing, but when I am rushing round on a busy day, how can I change how I see an atrocity on the TV news or when I witness suffering in my nursing work?"

Higher Consciousness: *"Alice, do not forget the 'battle' from your ego that you experienced was very physical to you and seemed to affect your whole body, but you maintained your inner strength and your presence of mind. You chose to see the Truth, that those feelings were from your ego mind and had no power and no existence. At that realisation, they stopped immediately as if they had never been. Your realisation was deep and true.*

Everyone has total authority to choose what images and experiences they put into the world. But also do not forget this is a group manifestation by a group consciousness. Therefore in this worldly ego experience, you will always encounter images manufactured not entirely from Love. If populations have much fear they will seem to empower fearful thoughts, feed them and manifest fearful happenings. This is not by outward choice but from inner ego's false core beliefs. Unless there is conscious manifestation, babies, children and adults do not outwardly choose the environment and circumstances in which they live, but on a deeper level, there has been a choice of what they will experience.

There is a group consciousness that generates the manifestation of images when the mass consciousness is either in fear thoughts or Love thoughts. The more people who are in Love thoughts, the more manifestations of Love will appear around the world.

All people are aspects and facets of you. You are all one; completely linked. So, and this is important, if you change your mind and wish to see, feel and manifest Love, everyone and everything around the world will be affected; the whole consciousness.

59

There is no separation between you and anything you see. Everything is an image the group mind has manufactured.

The more you choose to see Love instead of fear, hate, or anxiety, the more you will see Love reflecting around the world. Immense Joy awaits you!

It is a gradual cumulative effect. The mind is the most powerful tool given to you. Use it well."

Alice: "So when I am confronted by a horrific headline or event which takes me into shock and upset, what should I do?"

*Higher Consciousness: "Realise you are in fear. Feel the sensation in your body. Know your thoughts have taken a leap deep into ego. Tell yourself ego has no power over you and deny the negative power; deny the fear any existence. Do not deny the presenting scenario, **but deny the negative power it seems to have over you.** From this place of authority, state that you wish to see through your higher level of awareness, your Higher Consciousness, and **allow** this shift of awareness to occur. Feel the negative-fear state melt away to nothing, as it is nothing. Tell yourself with Truth, "Only Love exists." The image may still be there but it will have no power over you to send you deeper into ego fear. You have sent Love power around the whole world which will strengthen **everyone** against future ego thoughts and **will help everyone to deal lovingly with the presenting worldly situation.***

In a shocking event, once the fear reaction is dissolved, loving and compassionate actions can then follow. While the dream is still your so-called 'physical reality,' physical help in times of need will still be required. Give help effectively and compassionately, according to your capabilities, but know that beyond the apparent is the ever Perfect Peace of God.

*The more people that do this with **any** upset, the more Love thoughts there will be in the group consciousness and you will* *all move together into a higher state of being, full of compassion, caring, laughter and Joy. Fewer and fewer fearful happenings will materialise in the worldly experience."*

Alice: "Higher Consciousness, I have not been able to have my communication times with you for quite a few days as life has been busy. I have been having a fun, lively time looking after a young boisterous dog, but I have gone into exhaustion again. Even having a fun, joyful time I have become exhausted. Why?"

Higher Consciousness: "Firstly, your communication time with me is tapping into Source Energy which is missed. Secondly, your communion time with me loosens your attachment to ego. Thirdly, you are physically resting while communicating with me.

*The ego keeps score on everything, to throw at you at every opportunity. The ego keeps score on how much physical work you have done and reminds you that you have done more than usual, instills in your mind that you will be exhausted and this gives an expectation of this, so that is what you feel. At this stage you still have considerable belief in ego and **you will give your energy to wherever your belief lies**. Do not forget that while on this Earth, you and most other people are listening to ego most of the time and listening to Higher Consciousness much less."*

CHAPTER 7

WHAT IS ILLNESS?

Alice: "Please could I send healing for a friend of a friend with a brain tumour and would you show me how?"

Higher Consciousness: "Dearest Alice, of course. Tell me, what is illness?"

Alice: "From what you have taught me, illness is a thought of fear that has been repeatedly fed by the group-mind until we think it manifests and, as we live in our ego dream world, we see the illness as real and incapacitating."

Higher Consciousness: "What is the real state of being?"

Alice: "The real state is Perfect Love and Perfect Light as part of The Supreme Mind."

Higher Consciousness: "What is the world that you are perceiving?"

Alice: "The world I see is a reflection of my ego mind, full of doubts, fears and defences."

Higher Consciousness: "What is the world you could see if you looked through the Higher Consciousness Mind?"

Alice: "The world I could see would be reflections of Perfection and Love, manifested in a Blissful State as through Love's eyes."

Higher Consciousness: "So, isn't what you see and feel all a matter of choice?"

Alice: "Yes. If I truly desire to see beauty and Joy instead of fear and grief and I practice it frequently, this is what I will see around me."

Higher Consciousness: "Yes. Exactly; you are opening your mind to Truth."

Alice: "This explanation, as beautiful as it is, could be very upsetting and painful for someone to hear if they are crippled by a disease."

Higher Consciousness: "Yes, True Knowledge is always unsettling to the ego, which has built its false existence on deception. But the Truth is as a balm to their True Soul, which lies in wait of recognition.*

There is only one mind and this mind has total freedom of choice. Your Higher State of Mind has the ability to commune with you where you think you are, even if your thoughts are in deep despair and anguish, and to show you a different perspective. **But your Higher Mind must be asked.** *There needs to be a desire to be saved from this state and a willingness to let go of the fear that took you there. The tiniest glimmer of desire opens up wondrous possibilities.*

*If you see or hear of someone who is in the depths of ego and seems to be overpowered by weakness and illness, you can ask **for them** and with them, to see the situation differently. I will describe how this can be done.*

See yourself in your real True State as Perfect Love radiating Light. Know that this person is a reflection of you; in fact, they are you, as there is no separation. See them through the eyes of Love and see them as perfect, radiant and full of Joy. The illness was just a thought, an ego thought, and is not real and never was. Know there is absolutely nothing physical in an illness and it is nothing. See the illness melt into the nothing that it is and the radiance of Love take its place. Hold this picture of radiance and smile with it, laugh with it, cry with it in Joy. Utterly know this is true. Nothing in reality is physical. Therefore, releasing your belief in sickness changes what you are manifesting instantly. If you try to release your belief in sickness while your mind is deep in ego thoughts, your trying will be experienced as interminable and your goal unreachable. Asking instead, for your thoughts to be guided by your Highest Love Consciousness can dissolve mistaken thinking in an instant, and this is how healing transformations are seen. There is nothing the power of Highest Consciousness cannot do."

Alice: "That is wonderful, thank you. But (you knew there would be a 'but') what if doubt creeps in?"

Higher Consciousness: "There have to be 'buts' while you are still mainly living with ego thoughts. There will be doubts until you finally leave ego behind. It is possible and it is possible in an instant.

There have been some humans on the Earth who have truly realised this and have not entertained any doubt. That is why miracles take place. A few of these beings walk the Earth in your time; quietly but with profound radiance.

*The moment doubt creeps in, you will be dwelling on a fear thought, and this will influence how you perceive the world. **Let not your heart be troubled by your perceptions, experiences or thoughts that arise. Have no guilt; only recognise that there is a mistaken thought. Know that you are all innocent children of creation who simply had a childish thought that seems to have magnified.***

Be constantly vigilant and when there is doubt, instantly ask your Higher Consciousness to show you Love, beauty and Perfection instead. This will train the mind more and more, until eventually this will become the automatic way of thinking.

Practice, practice, choose and choose again. It is possible to truly see Heaven and Harmony here on Earth."

After my meditation today, I asked, "How can I help the whole world to live in Peace?", I was told to go and find 'The Course In Miracles' book that I had always intended to read and never had, and to turn to lesson 125. I nearly did not follow this advice, thinking, "This is ludicrous. This must be just my imagination." I did not even know there were lessons in the book, but I climbed up on a chair and reached for the book from a high shelf. Almost reluctantly and definitely doubtingly, I searched for the lesson.

In the lesson it says "This world will change through you..........." I knew the 'you' meant all of us, but I was struck dumb with amazement at the accuracy of this guidance! I could have been knocked down with a feather!

Later, very puzzled, I started to question, and was given more information.

Higher Consciousness: *"All change comes from within. Each and every individual changes the whole world with their thoughts, words and actions. Everything you do in this ego-based world is instigated with a thought, either of conflict or of Love. Everyone and everything is totally connected, therefore there are really no individuals. Every thought affects everyone.*

This is how the world can be changed! It can be changed by meditating on, or thinking of, the Oneness of Love that you are, and deciding to let go of imagined blocks to Perfect Love, Perfect Peace.

Every time anyone does this they will change the world!

This will then be cumulative and as more people do this, it will speed up the process."

My 'A Course In Miracles' book did not get hidden back on the high shelf out of reach but began to be explored as I tried to understand the profound spiritual concepts. The more I explored, the more I discovered there was a very profound synchronicity with the words I was receiving.

Life became busier and I stopped writing communications for some time and just enjoyed prayers, communion and surrendering to Highest Love.

Alice: "I have previously asked who I was actually speaking to and was so shocked and astonished with the answer, that I did not really take it in. Now please may I ask, Higher Consciousness, who are you? What are you?"

Higher Consciousness: "I am a state of mind far beyond mind. I am your original mind, beyond mind; the Original Love, the untouchable, non-graspable, Totality yet emptiness of Purity.

I am you and you are part of me. We are one. Yet to you, I seem a million miles away because you feel a chasm between us, a mountain between us, a universe between us, a thick fog between us. There is not even the thinnest veil between us. All there is between all humanity and I, is a thought; a thought that you have strayed and are not worthy to return. You never left me, my dear child.

I am you."

Oh, I nearly crumpled to a heap on the floor. Emotion burst straight from my solar plexus. My mind seemed unprepared for this and I was in a tumult of confusion. Up to this point I had felt that there were different levels of Higher Awareness and that I was communicating with one of those levels, not the Supreme

Consciousness. But now I realise that we have all been given access to the Highest Supreme Consciousness. When I composed myself, I asked, "But who am I talking to right now? Sorry to keep asking but this is so difficult to absorb."

Higher Consciousness: *"The True Consciousness that is endless. The Knowledge of Completeness."*

Alice: "Are you outside me in the ether somewhere?"

Higher Consciousness: *"There is no inside and no outside. There is no ether. I just am."*

Thinking about the concept of higher levels of consciousness within the huge collective mind, my logical thoughts asked what I thought was a logical question.

Alice: "Dear Perfect Oneness, are you the perfect evolution of the collective mind?"

Higher Consciousness: *"God has not evolved. God has always been;* **God is.***"*

Alice: "Who or what is the 'I'?"

Higher Consciousness: *"True Consciousness of Love."*

Alice: "Is there anything beyond the 'I'?"

Higher Consciousness: *"Yes there is the intangible, the unspeakable, the immeasurable, the inexpressible, the unnamable."*

Alice: "So has there been the slightest separation between the Great Unnamable and the 'I am' consciousness?"

Higher Consciousness: *"Only in concept alone. It was/is a tiniest moment of thought consciousness of 'Who am I?' which self-realised as soon as it began. It is over and yet still occurring as all there ever*

68

is, is this moment. The microcosm and the macrocosm are one, forever and now."

Alice: "Holiest of Holy. I thank you for this communication. I am so grateful."

Higher Consciousness: "You are thanking Self. I am you and everyone. You are communicating and joining with the Universal Self. One day, in what you perceive as time, you will all come to this realisation."

One morning, I awoke with a vivid picture in my mind, of a young woman full of joyful innocence, expressing and sharing her radiance with the world. I knew instantly that I must sculpt her. This would be a challenge because the image was to be life-sized.

After weeks of building a strong metal frame and months of sculpting the clay form, I wondered whether I was still following the guidance originally received, as I did not want to slip away from my clarity of vision. Preparing to continue work on this sculpture, I went through my usual ritual of meditating and asking to be guided by Love in my work. I meditated in the house, then in my workshop near the sculpture. I had created negative fear thoughts by worrying that the clay sculpture might collapse under its own weight and I asked that these fear thoughts be cleared.

Standing in front of the sculpture I completely surrendered to Love Source. I was taken on a stream of consciousness of just 'being' which seemed to encompass all time, starting in a swirling tunnel, then into vast, spacious Oneness, where everything blended;

nationalities, feminine and masculine, classicism and modernity. I had the strong impression of being on a still lake, then becoming the expanse of the lake. Maintaining my surrender to the pure beauty of Oneness, my body began to move, bending double submissively then being lifted back upright with absolutely no effort from me. There I stood in what felt like the most perfect balance while my hands were gently, very slowly, raised to waist height, palms upwards. What followed was an all-encompassing feeling that I was part of everything and everything was part of me.

I saw and felt the solar plexus energy centre of this 'Radiance' sculpture, and in silent astonishment, followed this as it spread throughout the whole statue. While I witnessed this, I felt a vibration run through my entire body until coming to stillness and repose.

Words did not seem necessary, as a calmness and reassurance was received.

I stood in wonderment after experiencing this, feeling in awe of the Power of Love that is waiting for everyone to simply request.

Alice: "Dear Supreme Oneness, how can I pray for a beloved friend who is going through a difficult time?"

Higher Consciousness: *"You may pray in words of these:*

Spirit of Supreme Love,
help me to see everyone's light on Earth as it is in Heaven,

equal in radiance, equal in Love,
as it is now, always has been and always shall be.

I see my brother/sister in strength of Love,
I see them in meekness of Love.

I see their fear dissipate like smoke and be gone as it never was.
I see their sorrows melt
and their happiness shine.

I do this for them, as they are bound and blinded in their fearful choices,
and little do they realise, at this time,
of the freedom in the choice for Love.

Love surrounds them,
Love fills them.

They are expansive Love.
They are Joy, they are Peace.

And so it is."

Alice: "That is beautiful, thank you."

CHAPTER 8

SEEING HEARTS

For month after wonderful month, I saw little miracles happening every day, four, five, or six times each day! These surprise miracles came in the way of seeing heart shapes everywhere! I saw hearts in marks on the sides of buildings and in washing-up water splashed on the worktop. On another occasion the water splashed and left a dry heart in the centre of a puddle!

Food fell onto plates in heart shapes when I served meals, a piece of cotton thread floated onto the floor in the shape of a heart and I saw hearts in the wood grain of furniture. Hearts would show up in all manner of unexpected places all day, every day! I kept smiling and sometimes laughed out loud when another one occurred. One day I did get a look from a passer-by when I gave a little chuckle at seeing hearts on the pavement!

I shared this with only a few people because much of what I experience would not be well-accepted and there was no logical explanation in the worldly sense.

I just enjoyed it and **marvelled** at it!

However the occurrence of these beautiful hearts suddenly stopped when I fell ill with mild 'flu. When I recovered from a few feverish, achy days in bed, I asked Higher Consciousness about the hearts and why had they stopped appearing.

Higher Consciousness: "Your heart was open to Love, therefore you were seeing simple expressions of Love everywhere. You were seeing almost everything filled with Love, therefore you were directing the way things manifested everywhere you went. Therefore, if you accidentally splashed water, it fell into a heart shape. If you were walking over pebbles there would be a profusion of heart shaped pebbles. This was proof to you that Love can manifest in what appears around you."

Alice: "Oh, how wonderful! I had not realised that. Yes, the more I think about it, what wonderful proof. Why did it stop suddenly when I was ill and has not restarted again now I feel better?"

Higher Consciousness: "When you took on that virus it was a choice to slip into an ego negative state. It was not a choice of your conscious mind but a choice from your many faceted, subconscious mind. This part of subconscious mind is composed of an accumulation of group-mind consciousness, feeding ego manifestations instead of Love manifestations. You must have subconsciously allowed the group ego to manifest as a virus. This shifted what you perceive as your personal consciousness in every cell of your body, out of harmony with Love. This is more evidence of the group-mind and Oneness with all."

Alice: "So why doesn't the virus stay with us and continue to overpower us?"

Higher Consciousness: "The group consciousness also has an expectation that this virus will last a certain amount of time and then diminish in power, and also a degree of expectation that Love strength will prevail. Where the group consciousness expects and believes that physical destruction will occur from this, then mass fatal epidemics or disasters will ensue. The outcome is influenced by your group consciousness, but not determined by it."

Alice: "Is it possible to overrule this negative group consciousness?"

Higher Consciousness: "Yes it absolutely is possible with the power of Love and the knowledge that all that seems to exist without Love really has no existence at all, then to choose for the power of Love instead of ego."

Alice: "But if this happens subconsciously, how can we prevent it?"

Higher Consciousness: *"Even when you were poorly, you knew you were being presented with a choice, is that not so?"*

Alice: I pondered. "Yes…. I did. Many times over those few days, I knew clearly that I had a choice whether to follow this course or not. I am sorry to say, I shunned the possibility of choosing otherwise. I did get the feeling I could have asked my Higher Consciousness to guide me, but I know I allowed the illness to run its course. I also thought, "Yes, I'll indulge in this little illness for a few days." I remember thinking that. Also because my strength was low, I did not have my usual resolve to always ask to see things differently, but I remember clearly having a choice."

Higher Consciousness: *"So you chose to give the ego the illusion of power."*

 Alice: "Yes, I did and I also know that once I had gone into ego, my decisions were much more negative than before. Previously, I had been tuning into Higher Consciousness every day, a few times a day. When I was ill, I remember thinking, "Oh, I just don't feel like doing that right now." I had immediately slid a long way down a slippery path.

This is showing me real evidence of the power of choices we make. I know this was only a simple virus, but it shows how easy it is to slip deep into ego then feel as if we have lost our power.

I presume a lot of people will seem totally unaware that there is a choice?"

Higher Consciousness: *"Yes. You were aware of these choices but most are made by the subconscious mind and are not in conscious awareness. Also, if people carry a huge fear of something occurring, whether an illness or a situation, and dwell on this fear repeatedly, they will unknowingly nurture the likelihood of the manifestation of this fear somewhere in their worldly illusion. What is perceived as major illness can take years, in worldly time, of distressed thinking before it appears to manifest into the illusion. It will have no reality, as anything not of Love has no power and no existence but will appear very real."*

Alice: "So if a person has slipped into the depths of illness and is feeling weak and disempowered, what can they do?"

Higher Consciousness: "Take the loving help that is offered in the world by fellow mankind and obtain appropriate medical treatment but also explore, with help if necessary, the inevitable long-held beliefs that have crystallised this condition into the perception.

Doctors, nurses, and alternative practitioners, are all part of the divine team at the level you currently perceive. There are also Love-Led techniques and methods in the practical sense that can be employed whilst deep in ego, to alleviate pain and suffering, thereby facilitating more clarity of mind. But the only way to clearly see Truth, is to desire to step out of the muddy waters of ego mind into the clearest ocean of Your True Mind which is at One with the Infinite Power of Love.

When there is belief in sickness, manifestations will follow the belief but, I tell you, your reality is complete happiness.

Everyone has a core belief and this is very deep, as the name implies. The majority of human kind carries a negative, false core belief, but it is not 'set in stone' and is movable.

The only way happiness will be felt is by giving up the dearly and deeply held false beliefs. This cannot be done from a mind pinned down by ego thought. So if happiness is your desire, go to your Peace, your quiet place within, where your integrity lies. Then, most importantly, ask to be in-tune with your Higher Consciousness, your Love-led state. Ask for help and have expectation of receiving gentle wisdoms. If you feel ready, prepare to uncover your false beliefs and expose them to the Light of Love where they can be dissolved like morning mist in the sun's rays.

Set aside time for this, as this must not be rushed. Ask yourself what troubles you. Then ask yourself what belief took you to this troubled feeling. Write it down. Then ask yourself what belief in you led you to that conclusion. Write it down.

Then if you are ready, go deeper. Ask yourself what belief, from your core, causes you to react this way. Write down what emerges.

Discover what is colouring the way you react to everything, and the way you perceive yourself. If you are able, do this exercise with a trusted friend to support each other.

At the root of this exploration, in almost all instances, comes the statement "Because I do not deserve complete happiness" and "Because I am unworthy."

Unknowingly, most people carry these thoughts as their core beliefs and almost all their driving force stems from this, interspersed with beautiful moments of feeling Love all around and feeling the Love that they actually are. Some people feel almost totally consumed by their negative beliefs and life for them is a continual fight and defence.

The core belief that you do not deserve total happiness

is a false belief.

Everyone deserves total happiness as their absolute birthright.

Everyone is loved and completely lovable. Everyone is a perfect child of creation.

False belief can be dissolved if you desire it to be so. Free the mind and go to your Peace, your place of utmost integrity and power.

Ask for help from Love-Led mind, from the Higher Consciousness, whether named in religious terms or not. False belief, fears and negativity cannot be dissolved using ego mind.

Make the decision to become free of false beliefs and proclaim a clearly defined statement of this in your mind or verbally. Ask Higher Consciousness to cleanse false belief from you. In your mind's eye lay these false beliefs out before you, willingly and sincerely. Ask to be given Truth instead.

Literally surrender in expectation.

Feel Love filling you and pouring from you. This is your True state. Do this often in the name of Love.

Ask for more and more false belief to be dissolved every day. Ask for Truth to show its shining face to you. Ask to feel the Truth of who you are. Ask to feel the Power that is yours. Ask to feel the Infinite Love that you are! Ask in complete surrender to Supreme Oneness and it will be revealed to you."

Alice: "Thank you. I am so grateful and I will try to work on this. I have much to let go of. I know deep down I feel like an unworthy wrongdoer who has sinned and continues to sin."

I wondered to myself how on Earth I could write about Love when I have made so many unloving mistakes in my life. I will need much help with this.

Alice: "May I ask a little more about the beautiful heart shapes? Now I have recovered from the virus, why am I not seeing hearts anymore?"

Higher Consciousness: "They would recur if you really wanted them to. You know that those happenings were not vital, but just a beautiful, fun demonstration of how manifestations of Joy follow the expansion and expression of Love.

You are being given lessons in the practical reality of Divine Loving Power and also in the inherent strength of decisions.

*You will see why these lessons are arriving swiftly for you, as the impetus for change is growing in momentum. You have been given these types of lessons all your life but have not been ready to assimilate them before. Normal everyday occurrences are all caused by the choices that are made although, up to recently, people have believed the world does things **to** them, when quite the reverse is true.*

*Every choice each individual makes for the power of Love changes the consciousness of the whole world because we are all linked. I say we, because I am part of the one consciousness and I am in each and everything and every person. I am just of a purer vibration than **you think you are.** But someday soon, you will all begin to realise Truth.*

I am a wisdom from all time and no time, and for eternity I have been waiting just to be asked to guide vibrations as they unfold. All anyone needs to do is ask how to see through the eyes of Truth."

I realised that although I understood the concepts intellectually, it was only the time spent in meditation that enabled me to feel the present-moment 'life' of the words.

The Supreme of All is an all powerful, living consciousness within us all.

I recognised that it was when I had the intention to completely surrender my worldly-will, however briefly, that I experienced the all-compassionate, wise, Highest Love Power, and that this was highly responsive and closer than the closest whisper.

CHAPTER 9

A VOICE OF AUTHORITY

9-9-09

Although I had not been writing down many of my received communications for quite some time, the usual process was for me to tune in to Higher Consciousness then ask questions. On this day, it was different.

As I surrendered to Love Source, I was instructed by a voice, which I immediately and instinctively knew to be of high authority, to get paper and pen to write. I reached to use the back of some photocopies but was told to get good paper, which I did.

This felt different, very different. I knew something important was coming.

Higher Consciousness:

"We come to you today to bring our great Peace.

Please set your mind aside and prepare for words of Love. Come to me open hearted, as a freshly opened lily. Lay aside past events that you think have tarnished you. Go within and know that all is still pure. Do not deny your rightful place in the cosmos of creation, for your rightful place is at the heart of Love. This is the seat of all creativity and all power and is given in equal measure to all.

The time has come for great change. This will be a very powerful change which has been long awaited.

At this time of change, many things will be washed away and many things will be empowered, so a new clarity will ensue. Do not be fearful as everyone will have a choice. The choice is for the Light or for a place of further great learning.

The time is ripening. The seedpod is near to bursting and the new seed are ready to spread far and wide to all the planes of life.

This will be a shedding of the old seedpod that has encompassed you all, while the seeds have matured. The seeds are bright, they are Glorious and they will shine triumphant.

Structures as you know them will crumble as the awakening of the new era is heralded in with Light and harmonious music.

This will be a glorious day, for homecoming is ever nearer.

Fear not my child, for all is orchestrated by the Grand Master and is already completed and you are all safe in the Master's arms."

I was left in stunned silence and the awe I felt was tangible. I needed time to absorb not just the words but the power with which they came. After a couple of weeks I gave copies to a local minister and a friend.

The implications of these words are huge.

I started to keep pen and paper beside me again in my meditations.

Alice: "Where did those words come from on 9-9-09, full of profound messages?"

Higher Consciousness: "This came from a higher place in your mind which is in communion with far higher minds. These Group Higher Minds are aware of how the mass ego mind is working. The mass ego mind is concerned with destruction, pain and suffering. For the ego mind this will ensue, as this is what it is fed.

However, there is a choice, and those who are aware may choose for Love, always Love.

Alice: "So how can the whole of humanity receive help to avert falling further into ego and suffering these things?"

Higher Consciousness: "Come into your Peace. Come into your Love Mind. Fear not. Many people around the world have a sincere and unbending wish to help the whole of creation, and from what appears to be your tiny place in the ego, you do not realise how humanity's task is unfolding.

Light is shining down on the universal mission and angels help every step of the way. More help is being prepared for when the time is right. At this time humanity will be told how to carry out the salvation plan with many minds joined as one.

The ego dream of destruction is being dreamed more and more, therefore the fear momentum is growing. But Love is stronger and ego is unreality.

Many like-minded people are gathering around the planet, with a willingness for good that shines brighter than any star. Their Love intentions radiate out like the sun and this will grow until its magnitude far outshines many suns.

Come closer to me every day. Share thoughts with me every day, until we become so close you will hear me clearer. You will feel my presence and my wishes and the need for words will be few."

28-9-09   I sat to meditate and surrendered totally to Love and Truth. As I drifted into a beautiful swirl of Light and emptiness, a communication of authority again swept through my consciousness; full of power, but bathing me in Love.

I was again instructed to write.

Higher Consciousness: *"All is peaceful, all is calm, but a storm is brewing, full of intensity. A great wave, a great surge will wash clean; will purge. It will come with great light, but fear not; all is planned and synchronised and not one detail has been overlooked. Every sparrow will find its rightful place and every blade of grass is loved equally.*

Even the bedrocks of power will melt and new power structures will form, based on Love. Waters will part and new lands form; lands that have been covered for many years. New civilisations will form and Love will play a bigger part. Love will still not appear complete, as this is but a stage in complete unification. Be not afraid. All is prepared and assistance guaranteed. Legions of angels, more than you could comprehend, are at hand, gathering as we speak.

This is an act of Love, not of revenge or punishment. This is a father showing a child how to walk. The child has to momentarily be unbalanced, taking one foot from the earth that is familiar and holding the father's hand. The baby does not fear. He wonders for the unknown and takes the step, safe in his father's arms. It is a natural progression. Fear not."

As I read through this afterwards, a tremor of fear rippled through me and multiple unpleasant scenarios arose in my mind. I had moved straight into ego, with a physical jolt in my stomach. Recognising this, I immediately stated that I wanted to experience this differently, through Love instead, and handed the fear over in my mind to Higher Consciousness. The fear and panic dissolved and I expressed a calm but quizzical disposition

Alice: "Dear Pure Oneness, Highest Consciousness, this brings up many questions. Please tell me, what should I do?"

85

Higher Consciousness: "Do you want to follow Higher Consciousness towards the Light, or do you want to continue to grasp possessions and follow childish dreams?"

Alice: "I want to go towards Light and Love, but I know I will falter. Look how easily I slip back into ego."

I sat in silence, not knowing what to think or say or do.

Later I plucked up courage to share this with trusted friends.

Alice: "Higher Consciousness, I am puzzled. Did I hear correctly, as I only want to hear words of Truth and Love? These very profound words, telling of tumultuous changes, have left me not knowing what to do with these words or even how to feel."

Higher Consciousness: "The words came to you from Power. From the only Power there is and has ever been. They came to you from Love. The words came to you from authority in the echelons of Power. Sometimes authority, and always change, when received into the ego mind, gives fear."

Alice: "I am trying very hard to remain in complete trust and not to waiver."

Higher Consciousness: "There are many people around the world who have received prophesy of things to come in your illusion of linear time and have received it with fear. If the people who have been chosen to receive, choose to feel fear, then this could become a lost opportunity, nothing more. This time of shift is imminent and great power is being made available.*

The Light-Workers on your planet are being given an opportunity to open their hearts to Love more than has occurred in many lifetimes.

If even Light-Workers choose to go deeper into ego fear at this time, then the planet will not rise with ease into its higher vibration on this auspicious occasion, but will continue to wallow in fear and perceived suffering.

God Power with such immensity is being transposed to Earth and can be used for Love or for fear. Those who cling onto a way of life based on defence and attack may experience their illusion deepening. There is always a choice.

How this power is used will signify how it is perceived and experienced. Light-Workers have been prepared and given opportunities for development all their lives, to open their hearts and help others to do likewise.

This Love Power is already being channelled with extra intensity to Earth, and the intensity will continue to increase. Now is the time for choices to be made and for dedication to the Light, and Love will come to fruition on Earth.

Light-Workers may come together to orchestrate synchronised and continuous receiving of Love and expanding Love to all, to ensure this intensified energy is used to empower Love and not to deeper entrench ego fears."

Alice: "How can we do this?"

Higher Consciousness: "Prayers and singing of all nationalities, cultures and faiths. Singing, praying and dancing, with Love and unity in your hearts, forgetting feelings of separateness and truly sharing your Open-Heart Love.

*Prepare peoples all around the world for increasing power and teach how to shed negativity and **welcome** the influx of power with Joy. Spread the word that decision time is here. The choice is to step into your true and rightful inheritance of Love or to* slide, as if out of control, deeper into the deceptive illusion of suffering."

Alice: "But many people will reject and ridicule this."

Higher Consciousness: "Of course, but at this time more beings than ever before will be ripe and ready. Even those who ridicule may decide to see the Light of change. Those who absolutely reject the Light may do so, but will not rise easily into the new vibration."

Alice: "How practically can I help? I live a quiet, almost insular life. I am not the right person to be receiving these instructions."

Higher Consciousness: "Dear Alice, it is not coincidence the contacts you have made. All the Light-Workers on your planet and around it are filled with more power than they could imagine. Just one person sincerely knowing they are Light, they are Love, they are Joy, and offering that with an open heart to others, can ensure a ripple action throughout creature kind.

All who seek happiness, may we uphold you and inspire you. Do not only sit and open your hearts while in prayer and meditation. Live it, take an open heart into the world and demonstrate it.

Spread the virus of Love and let it affect every living cell. It is not until every living being has made the choice for Love <u>within this dream</u> that this planet can rise fully into its new vibration.

*Prayers, thoughts and intentions can influence **everything** near and far. Time and space are no obstacle to the power of Love, as these are worldly concepts. Come in Peace all mankind, and accept your power."*

Alice: "If we are really already with you, Higher Consciousness, right now, why do I need to put information out into the world?"

Higher Consciousness: "It is correct to think you need do nothing, as you are still at home in beautiful Oneness with your Source, but you do not truly believe this. You believe you are in a sinful world full of trouble and strife. You believe things need correcting, and as you truly believe this, this is what you see and feel. So this is what you have to work with; your false beliefs, to gradually give them up, to let Truth shine through.

The world around you seems very real, and the reality of your infinitely powerful Loving-Oneness, like an unreachable fairy tale. People seem separate, all leading their lives in different ways. They are all facets of you and your thoughts. You are the ones who seem to commit murder and the ones who seem Holy and Pure.

By putting this information 'out into the world' you are helping your collective consciousness literally change its mind."

Alice: "It is my open-heart intention to let go of fears surrounding these huge global changes, to enable me to welcome them in positively."

I went into stillness and imagined my fears and reservations spread before me in the presence of Love. In my mind's eye, I laid them all out on a huge silver tray and asked the Higher Consciousness to take these from me and give me Peace instead. I surrendered. I visualised all these fears disintegrating into the nothing that they were and a smile crept over my face and a glow filled my heart. I felt so alive.

I asked if these scribbled notes about my struggles to shed ego thoughts and find Truth would be any help in a small way.

Higher Consciousness: "Dearest Alice, we know how you love to scribe words from us. On a Higher Consciousness level, these words are not necessary, as the Perfection-of-Now is known, but while in the lower consciousness state, these words are a helpful guide out of the darkness.

With our help, you may compile words of encouragement to help people open their hearts to the Love that they already are.

Come unabashed, unashamed and unfearful to us. Be not afraid of what you scribe for us. We love you and all of creation. These words come from Love and Light. These words are to help the Earth and all upon it to realise the true nature of all.

Bow down to Love willingly with Joy in your heart. Be absolutely sure that all is planned and will work out for the good of all. Bare your heart with no defences. Smile on all, especially those perceived as enemies. Forgive, forgive, forgive.

All is bright; all is light and this will be revealed. Darkness will be banished from all minds, as all minds will it to be so. Those who are ready for these words will see them clearly in the Light. Those who are not ready will see more learning."

I was booked to join a group of artists to exhibit my sculptures but had to cancel on the day, with huge disappointment, exhaustion and illness. I had been too busy every day for months, with outside demands made upon me, to complete my work or even meditate, and I had plunged into despair and ill health. I cancelled my exhibition for which I had worked long and hard, and went to bed to recover. I slept for a few days with fevers. Today I sat on the sofa with a blanket over me and asked for help from Higher Consciousness.

Higher Consciousness: "Alice, you have tried so hard to achieve and fulfil extra demands made upon you, always carrying frustration at not being able to do your beloved and desired activities. This frustration is based on ego and is wasting much bodily energy. You have been under the impression that your happiness relies on particular worldly activities and achievements. One day you will realise that this is not so. Happiness is an innate quality and does not rely on outward circumstance.

The basis to all this is: you want to make sculpture. We know that you want these sculptures to imbue and radiate Love to everyone and to open peoples' hearts. Your ego thoughts will do everything to prevent this. Have you noticed how life always becomes too busy to actually achieve this? If it was not this recent busyness and stress it would be something else.

Do not feel disempowered. Everyone has all the power of the universe available; it only has to be chosen.

The tasks presented to you recently were not negative tasks to be despised, but you reacted to them from ego anxiety, therefore you perceived them as obstructions to your life. To see these tasks through the eyes of Love would have presented them as just more of the beautiful flow of life. When you have no fear of being blocked from your happiness, you will see happiness everywhere and in all tasks."

I realised straight away that I should re-read the answer I received about fear of obstacles.

Higher Consciousness: *"Fearing you would not manage the extra tasks and fearing you would be prevented from reaching your deadlines, you became more tired, and slipped further into listening to ego. Without recognising it, you fed those ego thoughts, and of course, they played out as your 'reality' and you did not reach your deadlines.*

Do you see what happened?"

91

Alice: "Yes, I see. At the very first sign of discomfort and frustration, I could have watched my thoughts, where they were taking me, and stated I wanted to see Love in the situation instead of fear."

Higher Consciousness: "Your ego manufactured a scenario of illness passed on from a beloved visitor, at a critical time, who you could then blame. This could set up resentment between you and a loved one.

The ego mind is clever and will bring you down any and every way it can if you listen to it. You can choose not to listen to it. You can choose to laugh at ego as soon as it tries to fabricate ideas of friction and drama. You can choose to use your empowerment for Love, and you will start to see Love in everything!"

I asked Higher Consciousness to show me the Truth, and there, shining behind the illusion was the Joy and Peace that had been there all along. I started to laugh!   I recognised the futility of trying to find happiness in worldly goals and putting such importance on them. My gratitude for simple pleasures, and my understanding that all the satisfaction I could ever need is already here with me, filled me with even more Joy.

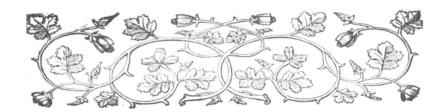

Higher Consciousness:

"Every day empower yourself with Loving Spirit.

Make this part of your nourishment;

Good simple food, clean water and Love empowerment.

Stretch every day and exercise lightly in a fun, enjoyable way.

Come to your Highest Consciousness every day and ask for empowerment.

Be aware of where your thoughts take you.

Any time you feel uncomfortable, go straight to your own Higher Consciousness.
Use your gentle breath and the power of your intention as a means to do this,
Ask to feel from Love instead of fear.

Practice, practice. This is the way."

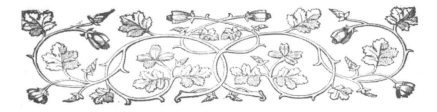

Sitting in the garden on a pleasant autumn day, I went to my place of Peace within my mind and asked to communicate with my Higher Consciousness.

Alice: "In our conversations I keep being told we *are Love*. How can I see the Love that I am?"

My eyes sprang open automatically and I looked all around me in a large arc, as if with fresh eyes. Everything I looked upon turned into the most beautiful thing I had ever seen. As I looked, even the mundane seemed iridescent, and of sublime radiant colours: the hedge, the grass, the fence, the concrete slabs, the washing line and the plastic pegs. Everything looked exquisitely beautiful. I was told, without words, that these images were composed of the Love that we all are, and that all images, when looked upon through eyes of Love, will appear full of beauty.

My ego immediately intervened and dragged me out of that beauty and Peace and I asked, "This is so very beautiful but what if I see a scene of pain or attack?"

Higher Consciousness: "If you saw those things, although they would be illusions, know that all illusions are powered by Love, as that is the only power you have. Everything is composed of the One Love Power, but the group mind chooses how that power is perceived. Metaphorically, it chooses which act, of which play, in which theatre, by which actors and in which disposition. If you see an attack, it is because you expect to see an attack, which is produced from years of conditioning, fear thoughts and accumulated mass consciousness."

Alice: "But I don't want to see attack."

*Higher Consciousness: "No, you have **consciously** chosen not to see attack, but you have many layers of consciousness: subconsciousness, group-conscious, and mass consciousness which are all influencing you. There are people in your perception who still do consciously* *choose to see attack out of curiosity, for entertainment, and from dwelling on fears which are then ultimately projected onto the images they perceive. I say 'them' but all is an aspect of you.*

*When you were helped to tune into Your Higher Self and saw everything, even the plastic pegs and the concrete slabs, as exquisitely beautiful, you were given a glimpse of how everything would appear if you **lived** through your Higher Consciousness even while in this Earthly dream. The more you practice seeing through Love's eyes, the more beautiful everything will appear."*

Alice: "This is my first day off for so long. Higher Consciousness, I am sorry I have been so busy and tired I have not been able to spend more than short tuning-in sessions with you, to feel the Oneness and listen to your words."

*Higher Consciousness: "Alice, do not regret the last few weeks. You have been interacting, relating, sharing and coping with challenges. Some challenges have nearly tipped you deeper into ego. You know you have been on the edge of reacting from a non-loving place and you have corrected that. Reading spiritual teachings and thinking Love thoughts will not enable you to fully progress until you have **experienced** choices for Love or for fear, and chosen for Love. This has been a valuable experience of making reactive choices minute by minute."*

CHAPTER 10

A FEW SIMPLE TIPS

ON THE PRACTICALITIES OF MEDITATION

Some people find it easy to slip into a meditative state then become open and receptive to their Higher Consciousness, but many do not. Do not be disheartened. If it is your intention to 'tune in' with your own Higher State of Consciousness for the benefit of all creation, then know that the **intention** is the most important aspect.

Physical relaxation and releasing of tension is required. For this you can sit comfortably and imagine any tension leaving your body gradually from the feet up to the head. Give time to this, as physical tension will reduce the feelings of your wonderful connection to Source. It is beneficial to sit comfortably erect with the back supported, not slouching. (You will feel the difference in the energies if you try both.)

Then it is of benefit to quietly observe your breathing. Feel the cool air rhythmically entering the nostrils and the warm air gently leaving. Gradually feel yourself rediscovering your Peace. It can feel as if you have found your inner cosy armchair. Sink into it.

You may find from this state of Peace, that you are ready to state your intention. Alternatively, you may feel you need a little more preparation to raise your gentle awareness to another more receptive level, in which case a beautiful visualisation can have just this effect. It may be helpful to record your voice slowly reading this gentle meander into a higher state of awareness. Leave pauses in your recording in appropriate places to allow you to enter into your Peace.

VISUALISATION

Imagine you are walking through a luxuriant green meadow. The sun is shining and you can hear birds. Meadow flowers sway gently in the soft breeze amongst the lush, green grass. Breathe in the perfume of the flowers.

You take a little path from this meadow which steadily winds up the side of a mountain. From here you cannot see the top but you know it is there in its beautiful majesty. The climb is easy, and as you leave the meadow you enjoy the clean air and the profound Peace. Near the top is a level plateau where you find a spring to drink crystal clear water. You walk over to a wooden bench, warmed by the sun, which looks inviting. As you sit on the bench you become filled with gratitude as you welcome the awareness that your Higher Consciousness is here with you; waiting for you. This is a time to just 'be' with your Higher Consciousness.

Allow the pure Love energies to mingle with yours until you are wonderfully filled with Joy, Peace and unconditional Love. This is your true state of being. You may like to ask your Higher Love Mind a simple question and state that you only want to hear from Truth, Love and Light. Wait in surrender and gentle expectation. An answer may come to you as if you 'sense' the words or as a picture, symbol or dream image.

In this peaceful state, full of Love intention, your ego thoughts may be quelled into stillness. But be aware, you may be required to repeatedly subdue busy, worldly thoughts and repeat your intention as the devious ego will always try to dominate. Gently instill in your mind a sense of timelessness and acceptance of 'what is' as you sit in surrender. Spend some time with this, enjoying the moment.

When you are ready to leave the mountain, visualise unconditional Love surrounding you and filling you. Know this will stay with you wherever you go, whatever you do. See this as a cocoon of light that you can radiate to all. Thank your Higher Consciousness and slowly start the descent down the winding path, knowing you can return whenever you want. Enjoy the clean mountain air as you descend. As the path levels out into the flower filled meadow, you become aware of the sweet fragrance, you hear the chirping of the birds and feel the earth beneath your feet.

Slowly bring your awareness back to where you are meditating. Feel the chair beneath you. Feel the floor. Recall the insights you have brought back with you, with a smile on your face. Take some deep breaths. When you are ready open your eyes.

As you start tuning-in to your Higher Consciousness with a loving intent, happy 'co-incidences' will start to occur. Fortuitous surprise meetings with like-minded people and unexpected opportunities **will** open up. The decision of the intent will open up more doors and pathways than you could ever dream of!

It is difficult when going through challenging thoughts and emotions, to remember how to bring the mind back to the uplifting and healing clarity of Truth. For this reason, I have formed an index of inspiring passages to refer to in times of need. (See back of book.)

If the words resonate with you, you can allow the resonance to sink deeper like a healing balm and allow the shift of mind to occur from the pain of ego-mind back to your True Mind of happiness and Joy. From here we can truly walk the Earth with a spring in our step and lightness in our heart.

Alice: "I would really Love everyone to be aware of these opportunities to be empowered with supreme happiness and not unwittingly use their choices to deepen the illusion of ego destructivity. I am thinking of people living difficult lives, fearing for their survival, in suffering or using attack. Please Higher Consciousness, how can these people be helped?"

Higher Consciousness: "They are all part of you Alice and you are part of the whole. Therefore, go to the darkest recesses of your mind, into your subconscious and lay out everything you find before me."

I surrendered to this and went deep inside my accumulated being. In my mind's eye I spread out a whole array of dark thoughts which looked like forms of matter; hard and spiky, mouldy, sludgy, and decaying dark slime, on a very large tray. I offered it to Highest Love for my dark thoughts to be purged and transformed. I went into complete surrender.

When thoughts crept back, I saw each piece of dark debris had been transformed to the most beautiful sparkling jewels! Diamonds, topaz, emeralds and ruby! I was overwhelmed with emotion, gratitude and wonder.

The realisation started to deepen in me that we can change the whole world by changing ourselves, as we are completely connected. The people we see suffering around us, are actually reflections of the unhealed parts of us.

This is something I will need to do again and again, as there must be deeper and darker recesses of my mind harbouring many more non-loving thoughts than I could be aware of.

"Thank you Pure Love Spirit!"

Alice: "What is 'Christ' or 'The Christ'? Even in non-religious spheres, 'The Christ' is often revered. Please explain."

Higher Consciousness: "The Christ is an essence; a pure 'distilled' elixir of God, potent and powerful with a flavour sweet and unequalled. The Christ is the elixir of life, available to all, through all time and no time. Jesus personified the Christ and realised the Christ Energy and Perfection. Jesus was a chosen embodiment of the eternal Christ Energy. Jesus was the Oneness within the perception of separateness for the purpose of leading back to Oneness."

Alice: "At what stage did Jesus become The Christ?"

Higher Consciousness: "It was always the intention that Jesus would manifest the Christ Energy, therefore he was the Christ from the beginning. Given his bodily incarnation into the ego realms of the worldly state, he could have chosen for ego thoughts instead of staying aligned with Love. The full potential for fulfilling his role of complete Love and Oneness was always with him, but his fruit ripened to become nectar for the world after many years of growth. At this stage he became a living materialisation of the Christ Energy.

Every part of humanity has this same potential to ripen into the Christ Consciousness. The difference lies in the fact that Jesus came to Earth with the intention of inspiring homecoming back to Love Source and most other living beings come to this 'material' state to separate from the oneness of complete Love."

Alice: "You said "Most other living beings."Does this mean, there are or have been others here on Earth that came with other intentions than that of the masses?"

Higher Consciousness: "There are many people who have walked the Earth quietly with the intention of inspiring Love and Oneness and have left their perfume on the Earth for others to marvel at."

Alice: "I know our function in the world is to be the Love we are and to shine that Love outwards like light. I also know our main role is to forgive, forgive and forgive again. But please Higher Consciousness would you guide me on what paths I should take; what career and how I should fill my time?"

Higher Consciousness: "Whichever way creation extends its Love outwards will be supported. Love is an energy, the only energy and whichever way Love is used, the angels will be there to support it.

If one chooses to extend Love through sculpture, all the power of the universe will be available. If a child of creation decides on extending Love by becoming a lawyer or a street cleaner, all the power will be available for that."

Alice: "But I have such a strong desire to do sculpture, should I follow this desire?"

*Higher Consciousness: "Well Alice, wants and desires will eventually fall away, but while walking on this Earth, step by step, wants and desires are inclusive in your experience. You have all been given freedom of choice and this will never be overruled. In contrast to the ego's fearful, anxious desires, whatever your **heart** desires when it is filled with Love will be a good and worthwhile expression for the whole of the Creation."*

Alice: "I recall that you have used the word, "lifetimes" in a previous answer, and I wondered if this referred to reincarnation?"

Higher Consciousness: "Souls may dream of different experiences, in a body, out of a body and recurring, but in reality there is one life, in a glorious continuum."

Alice: "Please would you tell me why some children are born with disabilities and illnesses?"

Higher Consciousness: *"Children arrive in this worldly illusion carrying their predispositions and ego burdens. They are old souls, borne into the world for a reason. There are no souls on this planet without a particular purpose. That purpose may be to stimulate more outpouring of Love and the opening of crystallised hearts throughout humanity. The spiritual heart is a powerhouse of Infinitely-flowing Love and heart-based wisdom.*

Within the world, many people experience this flow as staunched into a crystalline state. It is still full of its unique beauty and, like a snowflake, can be melted with the merest of change. It is the role of some beings to be that catalyst for change.

Some children arrive in this world having taken on a role of 'victim'. This role has been generated by the fears and expectations of the masses. But always there has been a decision made by that soul to willingly co-operate and join in the dance of wrongly-perceived unworthiness of the gifts of perfection."

Alice: "How can a child make these decisions?"

Higher Consciousness: *"These decisions are made on a soul level prior to manifesting into the worldly state as a cojoined sperm and egg."*

Alice: "What can we do for these children?"

Higher Consciousness: *"Always see the perfection behind the outward manifestation, and give all the Love and assistance you can to these children and their families.*

All are perfect children of Light, worthy of all the wondrous gifts of the universe."

CHAPTER 11

GLOBAL SHIFTS

I pondered on the words I had received about major global shifts and changes. After going within to my place of Peace, I asked "What will these changes entail?"

Higher Consciousness: *"The shifts will entail major change in the experience of the ego. No change is perceived without some discomfort through worldly eyes. The Heart will remain unchanged and untouched by worldly happenings. The True Heart of Love, the True Spirit of Existence is perfect now and always will be. The Heart is the expression of Godly Love."*

Alice: "How will these changes be heard or felt by us all?"

Higher Consciousness: *"Accompanying this shift will be an experience of longing; a longing to be free, a longing for a better life, a longing to be unburdened. This longing can lead to choosing again; choosing the true inheritance which is the birthright of all. Energy changes within nations will highlight this."*

Alice: "What can a busy, tired person do with this longing when they arrive home from work exhausted to face more chores and tasks?"

Higher Consciousness: *"It is so easy to slip further and further away, in the worldly perception, from what you know is true; from your true heritage, your authenticity. People perceive the life that ego-thoughts trick them into thinking they deserve, and this is played out in their worldly drama. Behind all false beliefs, everybody knows, deep down, that they are pure Love and Joy and this is what they deserve. Ego thought will tell them the exact opposite.*

105

The choice will be experienced as a father rousing his beloved child from a bad dream. Some will reject the awakening and continue in the dream.

Do not forget, everything you perceive happening in the world is filtered through the ego's perception; everything. When the eyes are opened they will truly see."

Alice: "So how can any of us see through these perceived upheavals?"

Higher Consciousness: "Few people in this worldly experience are seeing the Love in everything. Some will get glimmers of True Spirit, some are so embedded in following their ego unconsciousness that life on Earth already feels full of the troubles that they imagine and are trying to flee from.

This worldly experience is but a dream. Many, many beings are fighting for survival, grasping at everything on the way that they think will help them; possessions, money, power. Will this help them when they are roused from their dreams to enable them to awake?

If you are feeling the call already to a life of Love, then heed it. Prioritise quiet times even for a few minutes at a time, to connect with your True Existence. Feel the Love you are. Feel how that Love expands outwards, sharing the Love with everyone and everything. Judge not. Forgive. Do not hold onto grievances, small or large; let them go. Offer them immediately in surrender to the power of Love, to transform them into gifts of Peace and Joy. Know your brother/sister is you; part of the one whole. Know whatever you do to your brother/sister you are really doing to yourself. Know you are a perfect child of a perfect creation that in reality you have never left, but are dreaming you have."

Alice: "I would like to know why would The Supreme Being have put in place a temptation for us to fall from Grace into ego? But first I would like to ask whether I should even ask this question?"

Higher Consciousness: "You would not be on this Earth if you did not have doubts and questions. The ego has many doubt-filled enquiries to belittle faith. No question is unanswerable to the Spirit of God. This is a sensible question from the ego mind and it is not without reason. As you have a sincere desire to travel the path to Oneness, this is one of the ego's desperate ploys to pluck you back. The question is, what is your thought behind this question? It is to belittle God and God's plan. It is a purely ego question. There are times when Faith is what is needed and required to make that next step. Never fear. All will be revealed to you from the truly benevolent, loving God."

Alice: "Well, this did seem a sensible question."

Higher Consciousness: "So are you saying that before you fully pledge yourself to the path to Oneness, you must have this question answered?"

Alice: "Yes."

I was instantly taken on a journey of such clarity that all my senses were acutely aware of new surroundings and I gasped at the power around me.

Higher Consciousness: "You are on the edge of a precipice and you are hanging ever tighter onto the cold, steel, rusty railings that have made you feel secure. You are being offered Paradise. Now all that is needed is trust and you will fly. If you lean out over the edge, you may or may not realise, that God's hands are a fraction away from you, but you must let go of the railings before he can gently catch you and take you home."

Tears ran down my face as I realised that I was doubting, I was fearful, I was putting conditions in place preventing my total trust. Tears flowed as if from a deep well of resistance. Then through my tears I said,

"I will not ask this question."

I closed my eyes. I had just one hand on the cold steel railing. I let go and stood right on the edge. I felt a breeze blowing around me. I put my hands in a prayer position and in a shaky voice I pledged,

"I pledge to trust in God, The Supreme Oneness. I will not doubt your intentions. I put myself solely in your hands."

A tiny fear entered me as I asked, "Do I step, or do I lean over the edge?" fearing the plunge into the unknown in this hyper-real vision. But as I asked, my actual physical hands, still in prayer, were led outwards from me and as they moved they felt physically cupped by warm hands and my whole body felt as if I floated forward safely, beautifully. Profuse tears poured again as I said repeatedly, "I didn't fall, I didn't fall, I didn't fall......."

Alice: "I am sorry Higher Consciousness, I keep failing in my dedication. Although my desire is great, some days I seem to prioritise every conceivable task over my meditations."

*Higher Consciousness: "Dearest Alice, we come to you in great Peace. You are fulfilling your function. Each and every manifested being, even if you do not realise it, is The Light of the World. It is only a question of time in your world, until everyone knows this. Not just the deep knowing that is always there, but **living** the knowing in their manifest life. This time is creeping forever closer. Every time anyone tunes in to listen to The Highest Consciousness, the True Spirit Father Mother, with sincerity, this time is brought ever nearer.*

*We proclaim, that every time **anybody** sincerely desires and asks to hear the Truth of Love which is The Highest Consciousness, the consciousness of the world leaps towards Peace. There is no separation. All affects all. So be it."*

I had worked very hard and felt stress and dread prior to a four hour exam, one-to-one with someone I had heard was a fierce examiner. Finally, I sat myself down and uncovered my subconscious thoughts behind my stress and apprehension. My negative ego mind had been covertly building a terrifying thought that the examiner was a fine-tuned predator, stalking me in the bushes and soon to be right upon me. I had imagined the predator's teeth and unsympathetic eyes piercing me at any weakness. I imagined being ripped to shreds by a merciless monster. I had allowed this ludicrous, fearful, anxiety-thought to fester in my subconscious, generated by my ego mind and giving me a feeling of stress, with hardly any awareness that I was doing it!

This was a clear indication of how negative mind patterns can be generated in our subconscious which we unwittingly 'feed' and, if we allow it, they can then guide how we perceive the world, no matter what level of intelligence or rational thinking we may think we have. As soon as I brought this to my conscious awareness, I went to the bedroom so that I would not be disturbed, and asked to connect to my Higher Consciousness state. I asked for Peace and Truth instead of fear.

I visualised this image of a predatory monster, and in my mind's eye put this image on a very large silver tray, and handed it over to my Highest Consciousness. I surrendered to Love Source and waited.

Calmness washed away my fears and tension melted from my body. I was offered an alternative image of welcoming the exam with open arms and with an open heart and of welcoming the examiner as a good friend. I saw the examiner as a good soul, doing a difficult job in order to maintain standards and correct inadequacies for the good of the whole. I saw her with a friendly face and loving hands. I saw myself relaxed and loving towards her and felt a warm glow around the whole picture.

My whole attitude had changed just by seeing things differently, through Love instead of fear. My whole demeanor changed as I **wanted** to prepare my work well, without resentment but with caring instead. In a funny sort of way I started to look forward to my examination.

However, in my busyness a few days before the exam, I slipped back into fear and was too busy to go quietly upstairs to meditate and 'see things differently.' The next morning as I was opening the curtains, I thought I would go straight and feed the beloved wild birds, as it had been a very cold night. My first sight through the window was of a cat mauling a gentle pigeon and crouching beside the almost lifeless form. I banged on the window, thinking, "Oh I hope the poor bird did not suffer too much." Grabbing my dressing gown, I dashed downstairs. On reaching the garden I saw what looked like a small pheasant stumbling around. It was the pigeon, red with blood, in a terrible state and in shock. Its neck was very badly mauled and I looked with horror as I wondered how it was still alive. Dashing to the garage before the cat came back, I collected a dust sheet and gently wrapped the trembling pigeon; its eyes trance-fixed on me in fear. I kept saying to myself, "The spirit of this bird is in perfect harmony and Peace. This creation is safe in Love and Perfection." I made the wrapped bird as comfortable as possible in a box and drove it to a veterinary surgeon who said the only thing he could do was to give it a compassionate end. Later that day my husband reported hearing a crash on the upstairs window and I went outside to find another pigeon dead on the floor. It had flown headlong into the glass and destruction.

I contemplated these things after my exam and realised that after at least a year of not seeing any obvious bird deaths in our garden, could this be more evidence that thoughts we allow and feed, in our conscious and subconscious mind, seem to play out in front of us, seem to become our 'reality'? I had been fuelling such fear thoughts as these, of being attacked and mauled, chewed and spat out in my exam. Could I have manufactured those images that I saw around me?

I must resolve to go to my Highest Consciousness and ask to see things from Love, every time I feel out of my Peace, and not let it fester and fuel fear. This I know will be an ongoing lesson for me.

CHAPTER 12

THE FACE OF GOD WILL BE SHOWN TO ALL

Alice: "Please would you tell me more about the global changes?"

Higher Consciousness: "The people who have chosen to turn away from Love up to now may not walk easily into the Light, but all may choose again. The face of God will be clearly shown to all. Some will be so in fear that they will look away and flee into what feels like oblivion, but will simply be deeper into ego. Those ready will breathe the Peace of God into their very being and the breath will transmute the DNA structure and the RNA, changing humanity forever. Many children and young people already have primed DNA and RNA and the transition will be natural.

This age has been awaited by many generations for over 200 years, and has been in preparation for millennia. Come with fresh eyes, for you will feast on the new vibrations. Many of you are hungry for this momentous time. Open your eyes and open your hearts, for all will be revealed to you. A new heart vibration has been opening in many. In some it is in full flower, others carry this in bud. Far more have a seed yet to be watered and nourished. The time is drawing very close for the full blooms to flourish in Joy, Peace and Harmony."

Alice: I asked, "What is the difference between Jesus and The Spirit of Supreme Love?" (in Christian terms, the Holy Spirit).

Higher Consciousness: "The Holy Spirit is as complete as God, but is a role OF God and is literally The Spirit of God. The Holy Spirit, or Spirit of Supreme Love, enables communication universally with every part of creation wherever they feel they are in this worldly illusion.

*Jesus is as complete as God but is an extension **of** God, in the Oneness with the Holy Spirit, and has become **one with the Holy Spirit.** As Jesus manifested in the Earthly dimension, he has become a role model in some cultures, and a Love mentor with the Holy Spirit, constantly connected with every part of creation and vigilant for the intent of communication. He is in complete unity and harmony with other realised beings within the magnificence of The Spirit of Supreme Love."*

Alice: "Perfect Oneness, I am loving the teachings that you are giving me. The guidance shows me a different way of living based on simple, timeless spirituality and watching what we do with our thoughts. But how can I keep remembering these teachings?"

Higher Consciousness: "Hang this notice up in your workplace and daily living place so that you can glance up to it through the day and tune back into Love easily."

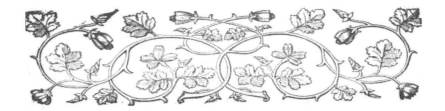

"Open your heart to Love and know it is overflowing,

Remember there is only Oneness,

Your thoughts go out to the consciousness of all.

They either deepen ego, or extend with Love.

There is no sin, just mistaken choices.

Forgive, forgive and forgive again."

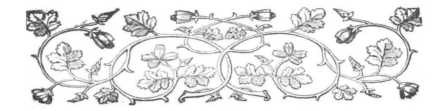

Alice: "What does the word Christ mean?"

Higher Consciousness: "The Christ is the Christian name for the Universal unalterable, Highest Stream of Consciousness, entirely composed of Love extending outwards, from eternity to eternity. It is the unalterable state of being of The Son/Daughter of God."

Alice: "So Christ was not the person Jesus Christ?"

*Higher Consciousness: "Jesus was a person in the worldly meaning, who truly realised that, as a Child of God, he is just Love, there is only Love and that this world is an illusion which can be changed in an instant. Jesus, therefore, embodied in the worldly state, in Christian terms, the Eternal Christ Consciousness or Christ Mind. He is a part of your collective dream and gives hope and leadership. In your world, he embodied the Highest Consciousness in action, and **he is an aspect of you all,** as everyone is a child of God the Supreme Oneness. This aspect he demonstrated by showing willingness to be open to Love, to surrender to the Oneness, to have lack of fear and to see the perfection of everyone. The smallest amount of willingness and desire to see Love in everything opens up huge amounts of connectedness with Source.*

All realised beings saw, and still see, the Universal Highest Consciousness everywhere, without exception, and thus became one with this Energy, which is named differently in different cultures.

Imagine this; you have a dream and it begins in a beautiful place, with loving people and is comfortable and relaxed. Then something happens in the dream to upset the harmonious picture. You feel scared and start to run. Then you fight and defend yourself and go into hiding, building a barrier around you so even the loving people in your dream are not welcomed in. Gradually you start to wonder if there is another way of being that is not defensive, that is not filled with guilt and lack. You peek out of a crack in your defences and see tiny glimpses of a beautiful green pasture. You wonder if it could be safe to open a window, but your fears make a vision of a monster hiding under the window. So you wait a whole lifetime in your dream.

All through the dream the loving aspect is still there, in you and in everything around you, and is The Universal Highest Consciousness. The fearful aspects are made by your own free will, which is given to you to choose. In every second you are free to choose to live through the Universal Highest Consciousness or through your lower conscious state. Both feel equally powerful whilst in the dream but in reality only Love exists.

*When you realise this, you will **know** that everything not based on Love cannot exist and has no power at all; this includes all fear, all illness and all pain. It is so utterly without power that you can visualise it crumbling to dust, and as the dust falls, it is **gone** before it hits the ground. This is healing; letting go of illusion and letting The Love of Universal Highest Consciousness shine through, whatever name it is called. It is very simple, but in your ego illusion it is not easy.*

Everyone knows, deep down, that they have full access to the Infinite Universal Power of Love, but most people are fearful of this and use great effort to conceal and block this knowledge. However, there is a dull ache of wondering in the background of the mind, which gives a searching restlessness in this world, unquenched by anything worldly.

*But know this; the Highest Consciousness aspect of everyone's mind **is already fully in tune with the immense power of Supreme Love** and can be called upon **whilst in this dream** to help loving decisions be made on a second by second basis. The Christ is a Love Inspiration; the Spirit of God within you."*

Alice: "What is the second coming?"

Higher Consciousness: *"The second coming is when humanity gives up ego negative thoughts, lives in and becomes the embodiment of the Universal Highest Consciousness or in your culture, The Christ Mind. All fears will have fallen away and the shining face of God is seen in everything."*

Alice: "Please would you tell me more about the changes which are imminent?"

Higher Consciousness: *"This is a time of great change. Intense training and repositioning in the field of conscious thought is required, and those most tuned-in and in peak training will be called into the team. Be dedicated, as every light-tuned individual will be required for the good of the whole.*

As you see changes occur, do not enter into fear. Protections against fear in the worldly sense will fall away. Keep a positive outlook and this will proliferate with those of an open heart. See beyond the manifested happenings of the world. Know without a doubt that only Love is real, and that the children of Love are being led surely and steadfastly back to Abba, Father Mother."

Alice: "How can I prepare for these changes?"

Higher Consciousness: *"However hard the wind blows, walk steadfastly on the path. Tune into Love Source every day as soon as you wake and as frequently as possible through the day and always before sleep. Listen to guidance. Wait for a response from Love*

118

Source in sweet surrender. Be vigilant for your ego responses to any situation. Hand over any fears immediately to your Higher Awareness and ask for guidance. Request to feel from Love instead of fear, and wait in silence and expectation as your heart opens again.

Know you are Love and that Love is infinite. Feel it radiating and extending ever outwards and being replenished in a never ending cycle.

Forgive all acts of attack and know the perpetrator is in a place of pain and feeling a lack of Love. Visualise them as the Totality of Love that they are."

Alice: "Higher Consciousness, I am starting to discover the beauty of the spiritual book 'A Course In Miracles.' Would you tell me about this book?"

Higher Consciousness: "This book has come through to help people walk the gentle path back to Truth. It is not totality, as that cannot be portrayed in words and writing. As far as Truth is concerned, this book may be eagerly consumed by those hungry for Truth and believed as anything written can ever be believed.

It is Truth explained in easy steps, as a lesson to a child. There is always more, as God's Kingdom is unfathomable, immeasurable. Great teachings are contained in this book 'A Course In Miracles' that may be consumed and ingested right into every cell of your worldly body and right to the depths of your conscious and subconscious mind. There is no need to fear any of the words in this book, as even misinterpreted minutiae are held in the presence of Love.

This book came through a reluctant but dedicated child of Light, in the hope that it will reach other children of Light to realise their own Light within.

There are other beautiful books of Light which have become soups; reheated, portions removed, leftovers added and boiled again many times. It takes a keen, discerning, untainted mind to glean the true nutrition from these.

Always follow your heart and be open to Love which will be Truth, as Love can only be Truth and Truth can only be Love.

If there is ever any doubt, open your heart to Love and ask, in any situation. Answers received from Truth will fill you with Power, Love and Joy."

CHAPTER 13

A VISITOR FROM THE LIGHT

With busy working days in nursing and running the home, I did not document communications for some months. Then on Easter Monday 2010 I had the house to myself. That was fortuitous, as I felt a strong calling to go deeper that day.

Alice: "I feel something is imminent. Higher Consciousness, I have so much to ask."

Higher Consciousness: "What you are feeling is the run up to………"

I felt this was so important that I slipped out of my Peace with a feeling of panic and lost my connection with Higher Consciousness.

With urgency in my voice I asked, "Please tune me in to Love and Truth, more and more. I only want to hear Truth." But I was far out of my Peace.

Higher Consciousness: "You are trying too hard. This seems so important to you today, that you are tense and over eager. You need to relax. Slow your breathing and go to your centre. Become Peace…………Just be. Trust…………Surrender………… Know you are Love………Feel your Love radiating outwards, never ending…………

Feel the Joy which is yours………Feel the Peace…………Become the Peace."

I surrendered.

Higher Consciousness: *"Wrap yourself in a cloak of Light and sweetness. Its sweetness soaks into you. Its nurturing is absolute. It is Love."*

I felt the golden sweetness. I felt the Love envelop me. I smiled inwardly and outwardly. Then in an instant realised the cloak extended out through not just our solar system but into never-ending eternity. Emotion filled me and tears rolled down my face. This brought me back to the room where I was sitting on the sofa, and I gently returned to my Peace and surrendered again.

I felt quivers and shudders. My eyes opened automatically and looked all around as if through another's eyes. I felt a presence with me. I was told that angels were all around. I stayed in my Peace in complete surrender and waited. While in this beautiful surrender I received a message which seemed composed of almost musical, harmonious words.

Message: *"We tell you great news. You may feast and make merry, for things are coming to pass which have been prophesised for many years. Great things! Hold not back, for Glory is with you, the Lord's Glory. Great things will come to pass shortly which will change the world permanently. Fear not, the Dove of Life is upon you. Bewilderment may ensue, but fear not. Let go of false beliefs, as these pin you into darkness. See the Light and always ask for the Light. Give yourself completely and in complete safety. It is in your giving and surrendering that you will be given.*

Fifth dimension work will come into full fruition, like a fully ripe fruit, delicious and sweet, full of colour and nutrition and this will truly feed you. Open will be minds to incoming wisdoms; although some will flee. Some are not yet ready for the big changes and have resisted signals from Love Source. It is their choice. Forget not that we come to you in Peace. It is for the benefit of the whole of creature kind that we come."

I tried to let this information sink into my meager mind and limited understanding, but I was in a whirl. I wanted to ask questions but was overwhelmed by the power and beauty with which this message arrived. I experienced a heightened awareness, of being held in loving arms. I surrendered into it, and as I did so, a persona came over me. Different facial expressions than I would use; smiles with puckered cheeks and lips. I was not sure what was happening. This persona felt female, full of Love, full of prayers and full of smiles but with a slight intensity.

Alice: "Higher Consciousness, what on Earth has just happened? It was as if a personality had just visited me. Was it from the Light?"

I was told that she is following guidance of Light and Love from a high spiritual awareness and is come to serve the greater good of mankind and all creature-kind.

Nothing like this had ever happened before and in my doubtfulness I put up something of a barrier to her.

Alice: "Higher Consciousness, should I allow this contact?"

Higher Consciousness: "This is a helper from Higher Realms. She is serving the Light every moment and has purely come to serve. Her willingness is great which gave a feeling of intensity, just as you were intense earlier today when you knew some message was imminent.

She was attracted to visit at this time, as you had just had a visitation by angels........."

I broke down in bewilderment....wonderment.... astonishment.

After quite some time, I asked Higher Consciousness if I could send her my Love, whatever dimension she was from. I gently lifted my hands and visualised my body being completely composed of Love which was expanding out far and wide and reaching her. I

123

visualised her as a perfect expression of Love, in complete ease, comfort and Joy. I held this beautiful moment for some time then I gave thanks.

I had a visit by some Mormons, who I invited in and they left a book for me to read. I read that: Jesus is the only way to Heaven and everlasting life. This statement of exclusivity perplexed me again especially as I am learning about the loving beauty of Buddhism at the moment.

Alice: "Higher Consciousness, are Christian books trying to imply that Buddhists will not reach the bliss of Heaven?"

Higher Consciousness: "Buddhists revere Oneness and Oneness cannot be named. Buddhists revere selfless Love for all. The fact that they do not follow and revere Jesus' teachings and the path that Jesus took is in name alone.

*True Love will always seek and find true Love. The sincerity of seeking to become Loving Oneness is the energy of the path, whichever doctrine is followed. They will not be prevented from reaching a Heavenly state as The Christ Consciousness is just one name of this beautiful truly universal energy pathway which opens the way for **all** led by True Love. It is nameless and without doctrine, but it is the way. It is not embodied, it is not material as 'material' is energy materialised into a thought-form."*

This was a mind blowing revelation to me. I have explored many faiths and rejected parts of most of them and disliked any implied exclusivity. I have searched for that very pure essence underlying them all. Now I am being told that there is **one pathway** towards Unconditional Love that all faiths take if they strive towards True Love. The pathway will be named differently depending on which faith or doctrine but it will be the *same energy pathway.*

I also read in the Mormon's book about 'the straightness of the path and the narrowness of the gate' and asked if this could be explained.

Higher Consciousness: "The narrowness of the gate is because guidance on living a life of True Love contains few words, and the needs are simple. It is human ego that has complicated things with its complexes and complexities, its desires and its drives. The path is as narrow as it is Pure, as Love is the only way. Love your neighbour as yourself. This encompasses all, and all of life."

Alice: "I also read a passage which says that, "After baptism and receiving the Holy Ghost, and speaking with a new tongue, if you then deny me, it would be better for you that you had never known me." Please would you explain what this might mean?"

*Higher Consciousness: "People who fall from grace often fall into a place of their own imagined suffering. This is because of choices being made from a place of fear instead of Love. This is true in the worldly experience. After experiencing the joys of living in Grace, experiencing a life where a choice is made to block the Love of God will feel like hell. This is true in the worldly experience. It is not true to say, "It would be better if you had not known me", but this is how it could be **felt.** Ego mind will always try to build and reinforce guilt, but there is no sin, only mistaken choices, and guilt is a yoke not worth carrying. Guilt can be left by the wayside and be gone, as you walk in the Light of the Truth that everyone is, in absolute reality, an unalterable Child of Light."*

125

I asked for insights about clusters of little beetles around my kitchen window sills that I had traced to a bag of cheap rice. I did not want to kill them, but they might have invaded other items of stored food and I had been painstakingly carrying them outside on pieces of paper. (I had also been wondering about my vegetable seedlings being decimated by slugs again.) I waited for a response. As I had been in the middle of tidying the kitchen I did not write this as it came, but this time had to rely on memory.

I was told that the creatures were destroying the good food; the food stored in the house and the new shoots of life-force and nutrition in the garden. The food represents nurturing, abundance, Joy and energy. I was told that if I do not feel worthy of all the Joy on offer, then the ego mind **will** produce some obstacles to Joy and abundance in order to play out what I feel I deserve. Also we must bear in mind that this applies to all walks of life: jobs, relationships, fulfilment etc! My guidance went on to say that the opposite is true, that if we accept our rightful place as perfect children of creation, and always see the perfect Light in everyone, then what we see around us will reflect that in beautiful harmony.

As most of the time I do not feel very worthy, I realised that, in relation to food and abundance, I was subconsciously self-sabotaging! I was told that this of course applies not only to me, because everyone is part of the one-mind and everyone is linked in a dance of life.

But the wonderful thing is that we can turn this around! We are not passive pawns in a chess game; we are decision makers! Some things we can turn around immediately by changing how we think, other things we discover we are not yet willing to let go of.

Later I sat down, remorseful because of the damage I may have caused to the beetles as I swept them up, and I sent a thought of blessing to them. I tuned in to Higher Mind and asked for guidance.

Higher Consciousness: "Do not be despondent. To continue to function well in the world with the level of belief you presently hold, you will need to address worldly tasks. The illusion you seem to inhabit, is almost entirely constructed of insults and assaults, defence and attack, and you are not yet willing to leave this illusion behind.*

It is not possible, whilst in the ego illusion, to live a life without harming another part of the illusion. Just by digging the soil to plant seeds you will be harming multitudes of organisms, whilst in this dream. All that is asked is that you do the best you can in the circumstances presenting to you. Give compassion, and honour those life forms, for they have manifested and revealed your belief in suffering, enabling you to ask to see Truth instead.

This is another example of nurtured thoughts being manifested in the world and can be likened to the manifestation of hearts when you were filled with Joy.

Whatever anyone perceives in their experience is a useful indicator of the level of consciousness that is currently being chosen, according to their beliefs.

If you perceive suffering anywhere, you are carrying a belief in suffering and unworthiness.

Be gentle with yourself. You are not expected to take a huge leap of faith and experience a change of belief instantly, although this is possible. While you are transitioning you will still encounter tasks that appear distasteful, which seem to be necessary for functioning in the world. Even while incongruous tasks are being carried out, hold in your mind the intention of realising the congruous loving nature of all. The experience of encountering incongruous tasks will then become less and less as the True Nature of All is revealed.

Accept where you are with no guilt and no judgment of yourself or others. Know that you can change your whole world by *choosing not to give ego negative thoughts any room in your mind, and choosing thoughts based on Love instead. **As less belief in guilt and unworthiness is held, belief in happiness and Joy will shine through.***

Do not forget, this change in belief cannot be done from the state of mind that gave you that belief. You will need to go to your Higher Mind, your Higher State of Awareness, and state your intention. When you do this, eventually you will only see Love and Joy played out around you. These are the choices that have always been available. Watch your thoughts and use them wisely in this time of empowerment."

Alice: "Thank you. This is quite funny. Every time I have asked about slugs, I have received amazing teachings!"

Alice: "What is blocking our readiness to accept the transformation back to peace?"

Higher Consciousness: "All that blocks your readiness is your false belief of your unreadiness and your repeated imaginings of this."

CHAPTER 14

DANCE TOGETHER AS NEWLYWEDS

Thinking back to the visiting personality from the Light, I asked to be told a little more about her.

Higher Consciousness: *"This visitor is of Godly Mind, well tuned and ready for work with the Light. She has waited and watched, ever willing and vigilant for your readiness. It is safe for you to work with her and she is always surrounded by angels."*

Alice: "Higher Consciousness I only want to work with Truth. Will it benefit the whole of creature-kind to strive towards the Light if I work with her?"

Higher Consciousness: *"Truth is Truth and I tell you this visitor is working closely with Light, as close as you can be expected to reach in this moment of your worldly illusion. Yes, work with her if it is your wish."*

Alice: "What should I do?"

Higher Consciousness: *"Open your heart. Have no fear. Have Light and complete Love in your mind and it will come to pass that you will experience co-operation on a level not experienced by the ego-led mind on this brink of dissolution of dark thoughts, and a quickening of desire for Love will flow like a silk ribbon from a never ending spool."*

Alice: "What should I do now?"

Higher Consciousness: *"Await the arrival of your visitor from Light."*

I drifted deeper into my Peace and felt the persona come over me and join with me.

Alice: "Are you with me?"

Visitor from the Light: "Yes."

Alice: "Why have you come?"

Visitor from the Light: "I come, my child, because of your great desire. I also have the great desire that you experience; to bring the group consciousness out of the darkness and into the Light. There are many Light workers like myself. All want to match their desires for the Light with an 'Earthly' soul and dovetail in harmony, to work together beautifully, like two watercolour paints mingling to make another even more beautiful colour. Have no fear whatsoever. "

Alice: "I have no fear.

I felt some tension from you as you arrived, just as I felt on Easter Day when you visited."

Visitor from the Light: "This tension you felt as our energies merged is because I focus completely on the Light and on my reason for coming which gives me utter Joy and Bliss. But as I slip my energy into yours, the ego fears that you still hold, that keep you in the illusionary body, give me a slight altering while I merge with ego mind."

Alice: "Higher Consciousness, I do not want to be deceived and I do not want to deceive myself. Is this happening?"

Higher Consciousness: "There are different dimensions and ways of accepting Love. It is useful to bring a slightly higher acceptor of Love to greet and help a novice. You will teach each other as the challenges the 'teacher' encounters is also a learning experience. If the goal of the two is Love and that is held supremely, the road will be paved with Love for the whole of the One Mind."

Alice: "Thank you. May I talk with you, my welcome visitor of Light?"

Visitor from Light: *"Yes, I am ready to listen and accept anything you say."*

Alice: "Do you have a name?" I felt a name was important, but this made me tense up and I lost the connection briefly.

Visitor from the Light: *"Let us not do name at the moment. I want you to feel completely at ease with me."*

Alice: "How can we together help the one consciousness to drop away negative ego thoughts, including my own?"

Visitor from the Light: *"Let us just merge comfortably for a while. Let us float together and feel the little eddies and ripples. Let us feel the surges and waning of our energies together. Let us feel the beautiful colours as our vibrations mix. Let us dance together as newlyweds. Let us walk together along the border of sorrow and Joy and know which way we are to go."*

This was an indescribably beautiful time of joining. My hands automatically glided lovingly over my body and face. It was healing and tender as I welcomed her and she welcomed me.

Alice: "Will you always be with me now or will you just come when you are requested? And will you be able to help me deal with my ego thoughts in everyday life, or will it just be for more special reasons?"

Visitor from the Light: *"Oh daughter, sister, what wonderful learning we both have ahead of us!*

Any *thoughts of Love instead of ego fear give Love to you and to the whole of creation! Whether it is a simple thought of leaving the vacuum cleaner out to show your husband you have done some housework or putting it away, saying nothing and just loving him instead. Even that thought for Love sets in motion Love all around the group-mind."*

Alice: "Oh, you have been watching me." I laugh. "I do leave the vacuum out, and I know it is an ego thought when I do it, based on fear of being thought lazy, but I still do it! I will try to change that."

Visitor from the Light: "I have been with you for a long time. If you want me with you I will be there. We have much work to do."

At this I just melted into receptive silence; not questioning, just peaceful.

A joining, a mingling, and words had no importance.

Alice: "Spirit of Truth, I have just read some chapters in the Old Testament of The Bible and I am distraught. I want to understand and gain wonderful teachings from it as many around the world do, but I find parts of The Old Testament unsettling. It contains such angry, vengeful words, allegedly from God and full of punishments and violence. It upsets me so. Help me. I am so puzzled!"

Higher Consciousness: "The heart energy was not developed and evolved to the extent it is today. Peoples were mainly driven by survival energy, not Love energy. It was still very much in the depths of 'the fall'.

The lower energies ruled their minds and actions. Therefore all they perceived was gross and base, even their perceptions of the Supreme Power of All was filtered and corrupted by the gross ego state they were in. Even the seers of the time were under the grip of these ego perceptions. This meant that sensory perception and intellectual processes were based almost entirely on fear. Rather than the 'Old Testament' being seen as a dichotomy of the word, it is a true example of the low and fearful mind set of the time; so deep in ego that even spiritual experiences were wrongly perceived as fearful renditions from a violent God, when heard and seen through gross ego minds.

God has never changed. He/She is loving and always has been. The human perception is evolving and therefore words from God are now more often heard and perceived with less fear and received with Love, as they were always intended. If people want to remain stuck in fear, reading words of fear, they may, as there is free choice, but evolution of consciousness towards Love is inevitable. For this, people will pick up more appropriate tools, more based on Love, but they must always be discerning and use intelligence and wisdom on their increasingly Love-guided paths.

Ask to be tuned into Truth, Love and Light. Give time to this and do it often and from that place ask for guidance on paths, the written word and practices. Open the heart and be discerning with the heart, as the heart is always linked with Supreme Love."

Alice: "There seems to be one disaster after another happening around the world. How should I react when I see and hear families in difficulties?"

Higher Consciousness: "All, including children, the elderly and the infirm, have a choice and on a deeper level than visible, the choice has been put to them. Everyone, whilst still in spirit, has chosen which life transforming situations they will allow, within the worldly illusion. These choices are deep within the subconscious mind and are not easily accessible, but can be changed by choosing again.

Some have chosen to follow fear at all costs. Within your ego framework, this is difficult for you to understand. None are victims, although they appear to be. When and how worldly life is experienced is chosen.

Be compassionate and do all you feel capable of doing for others. But know that beyond all perceived suffering, all is perfect. Love one another and do not despise choices others make. Love, forgive and always trust in the Highest Truth. Share what is given to you as more will be provided."

Alice: "To what degree share what is given to me?"

Higher Consciousness: "Share what is comfortable for you to give. Some enlightened souls will be comfortable to give all. Some will not be ready to do this and will fall into fear if expected to. It is not helpful if one of God's children tries to leap forward onto what they perceive as unstable ground. Better to recognise the self-imposed limits of their comfort zone than to fall into fear. This will be something to open the heart to later. You should do what your heart tells you to do, as and when you are ready."

Alice: "How can I help people who seem unconscious of the power of choice and of our homeward journey?"

Higher Consciousness: "There are messages, signs and angels in abundance, but many do not see them or are fearful of them. Every single time you tune in to Love Source sincerely, everyone and everything is affected. If you have the courage, you can speak of reacting in Love instead of fear; but I know you do not find it easy to speak of these things. There are many souls now who are simply sleeping and can be gently roused with the merest whisper."

Alice: "Higher Consciousness, the profound words I have received about huge shifts soon to happen; who or where did these words come from?"

Higher Consciousness: "These words came from One who knows. This knowledge comes from a pure place where there is no vengeance or destruction. The words were not forecasting any pain or devastation as in reality there is none of this ever and never shall be. This world you experience is but a dream."

Alice: "But these words are foretelling difficulties and potential suffering **in our dream** which we will experience as real. Why do we have to bear this? Why not wake us gently and guide us in your arms back out of the dream and back to you? Why does the world need to suffer difficulties?"

Higher Consciousness: "The words were telling of the choices that have been made, and still are being made, in your ego world. But people can choose differently and their choices will be empowered. Further empowerment is coming and it can be used for opening the eyes and seeing the wondrous beauty of Truth and profound happiness, or for deepening the ego dream which could be perceived as suffering.

You will need to reclaim your position of Light voluntarily. It will never be imposed upon the Children of God while you stumble on, determined to maintain false beliefs. You are being offered endless choices; chances to accept the Love that you all are and the total Perfection of Creation.

The 'time' is right for change. Some are leaving the ego dream consciously in the realisation of its falsehood and walking into the magnificence of Open Hearted Love. Some walk the Earth but are not of the Earth.

Please do not forget, this is a dream and you are all safe in the arms of Oneness even now."

CHAPTER 15

GRATITUDE

A family member has had a wonderful healing from a very severe injury. Absolute Joy and gratitude bubbled up in me about this as I stood in the kitchen preparing an egg sandwich lunch. My gratitude was so immense that it outpoured as gratitude for everything: my family, good food, health and all provision in life, including the simple sandwich in front of me. I felt raised up into a state of extreme Joy and happiness.

Then suddenly, wham! My thoughts turned to the egg and the suffering of the hen!

Alice: "How could my intense Joy turn so quickly to grief and sadness?!"

*Higher Consciousness: "The clever ego part of your mind finds it difficult to tolerate Joy and gratitude. Even in joyously contemplating the gifts of life around you, including the simple sandwich, the ego diverted you into grief. The ego part of your mind will always try to divert you into fear and guilt. You were **so** extremely grateful, with tears of Joy welling in your eyes, that you were diverted to **the direct opposite**. See how swift is the clever ego mind."*

Alice: "Please guide me in Love. What would Love think about eating a free-range hen's egg and the lifetime of service to humanity by the hen before, possibly, a violent end if it is slaughtered?"

Higher Consciousness: "Dear Alice, the hen was not a victim. All is a manifestation of internal thoughts. All is a manifestation of a fragment of you and the choices the collective 'you' make. The collective 'you' is the whole of the manifested universe that you ever perceive. The hen is a part of you that chose that experience. Some choices are to experience being a battery hen and all the hellish conditions; some choices are to be a free-range hen but still experiencing a 'bitter end'. This is symbolic of how the ego perceives this world i.e. that all experience suffering, then die. In reality true life is beautiful, perfect and never dies."

Alice: "How can I see Joy in this without ignoring or condoning suffering?"

Higher Consciousness: "If you have not the intention of causing suffering, but have, in the worldly sense, inadvertently caused suffering through ignorance or lack of thought, this would have absolutely no guilt attachment. If you have reached a state of searching for purity and still choose to participate in whatever you perceive as cruel, this is a choice to punish yourself with guilt, as punish yourself you will."

Alice: "Is there any way of enjoying a free-range egg and even being joyful at knowing that the hen would possibly be slaughtered at the end of its productive life?"

Higher Consciousness: "There is no way of feeling total Joy at anything in this world, as up to now, this world has been seen through ego which is not Truth and is illusion. Everything has to do with the intention in your heart. You could go through life not caring if you harm, stifle or oppress. But what would be in your heart would be a callous disregard for your brother/sister creature. This could not bring Joy, only more self-punishment and many, many more chances to choose for Love instead. The path to Joy is paved with the desire to Love your fellow creature as yourself. But please do not go into guilt. Guilt is an ego ploy, put into the mind to obscure the Perfection of all Creation's Children. Acknowledge and utilise the Universal Divinity given to all, as far as you are able, in your current level of consciousness. Whenever you are not at Peace with yourself and with your surroundings, invoke your Higher Consciousness state and ask for guidance. It is always available, closer than a whisper away, and longing to be called.

Gently and gradually, remove yourself from being part of intentionally instigating and perpetuating suffering, and mental punishment on this matter will cease. For some while you will still observe unloving actions going on around you, but you will feel no part of it. Accept that other parts of your collective ego are still choosing to punish themselves and obscure the natural state of Pure Joyous Peace.

Just Love them and accept them for the Perfection that they are beneath the outward expression."

Alice: "Please may I experience the extreme Joy and gratitude that started this conversation today."

Higher Consciousness: "Know that Joy is all there really is, as one of the expressions of Love. This is what you are and what everyone is. For a moment you unpeeled your armour of ego, allowing you to experience the real existence of all. Sit for a while and unpeel your armour against your True Self."

A healing sequence followed where I completely surrendered to Love Source, which gave me profound Peace and allowed my Joy to come forth. A Joy so immense, it was as if my heart was outside my body and I was lifted in silent communion with Oneness. All human frailty and mistaken thoughts seemed to dissolve as I was held in indescribable ecstasy and wonder. It felt as if I danced, sung, flew, laughed and that all wondrous things were possible!

When I think back to the dream I received which was described at the beginning of the book, I find myself pondering, "Who was the other person receiving at the table?" and the slightly comical, "Why did they receive the whole juicy melon and I the stalk?" I think we were representing humanity and that we could choose and accept wholeness here and now, but some of us tentatively choose only part of wholeness, not feeling that we deserve completeness and totality. This made me smile as I remembered a spiritual teacher saying, "If you had the choice to go through the door to perfect happiness or through the door for more and more lectures on happiness, which would you take?"

This left me wondering........

It was February, and I looked up at our eight foot tall yucca plant in the garden. It was looking very damaged after the extremely low temperatures of the winter and was just a bedraggled bare stalk. With sadness I thought, "Poor yucca, will you survive this?"

I immediately felt a surprising response, "We will survive in spirit forever. Do not think of us as this one plant, as we are part of all the yuccas and they are part of all the plants and they are part of all of creation. Do not be sad. Always think of the unity of all and the cycles of this manifestation. We do not feel sad as we are not connected to the part of mind which holds sadness."

CHAPTER 16

ALL IS PERFECT NOW

I came to Higher Consciousness in grief at the recent catastrophic devastation in Japan and desperate for some message to put out on the internet worldwide to ease the grief of all mankind. I was very affected by the response.

Higher Consciousness: *"Your message to 'save the world' is not needed. The True Creation is as it should be. If the body or your surroundings seem to be less than the Perfect Expression of God, know that it is your perception which is distorted. Know that everything that is presenting to you is how the collective-you is choosing to perceive it.*

In reality all is perfect now. If people are choosing to see The Divine Kingdom as physicality, then that is how the Divine Kingdom will present, radiating the Totality of Love from every particle. If this choice for physicality is also chosen to be perceived without Love in the mind, then physicality will be perceived as difficulties, obstacles and trials. However, the Perfection of The Kingdom of Heaven, in reality is all there is.

There is nothing to fix. ***There is nothing outside yourself.***

Many will not feel ready for this statement, but some will be. Behold those who are ready!

The fears of the world which you want to 'fix', are all inside the mind, manifesting visions of destruction."

An artesian well of emotion erupted in me with much sobbing and crying, like a volcanic outpouring from deep within my being, as finally, finally the tiniest glimmer of realisation was coming home to me.

All my working life I have been in nursing and therapy work, but always my intention was to 'fix' something that was wrong. Finally I was beginning to understand that we can give Love in thoughts, words and deeds, but attachment to the outcome of 'making the world better' is misplaced. If we see imperfection it is only a projection of the lack of Peace we feel within. There is only a *thought* of imperfection which comes from a mistaken belief, and that thought can be thought differently, by realising there is only Oneness and Perfect Love, nothing else. But through my tears, even after this revelatory moment, my ego started to fight back and wanted 'Something, something!' to help the world.

"If there was a message I could send from you, Higher Consciousness, what would it be?" I pushed.

Higher Consciousness: *"All is Perfect. Love is all there is."*

Alice: "But if I said, "All is perfect," many people will not understand. Is it feasible to have a message of help while we are still in this illusion??"

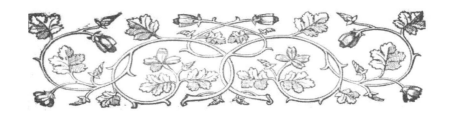

Higher Consciousness:
> *"Believe in Love.*
> *Do not believe in fear.*
>
> *Do not give fear any room in your mind,*
> *for fear breeds more fear and images of destruction.*
>
> *Be firm and resolute.*
>
> *Say "no" to fear and Love will sweep the Earth,*
> *harmonising and restoring.*
>
> *Now is the time for this change.*
>
> *Open your heart*
> *Let your Love expand to all."*

Alice: "Thank you, that is beautiful."

Alice: "Please Higher Consciousness, may I ask for words of Love and wisdom for a friend who very passionately wants to help humanity?"

Higher Consciousness: "Dear Alice, your friend is a good soul. She feels she has come with many tasks and the weight is heavy.

All preparations over eons of your time are culminating now in these times. Much work has been done in preparing the psyche for a time of decision.

Your friend has intellectualised what she sees as stages in enlightenment, has fought to educate and fought to change circumstances. Her passion is driven by fears for humanity and she is full of fight, but fighting will not help her cause.

This time is a time of rapid change. It is time to move to the next level, where the fight has turned to Love and this is the driving power instead of the force of fear. This is a time when Joy shines forth and struggle and strife is put away, like a child's fearful dreams. This is a time for maturing into the Oneness that is the Perfect Perfection that has in reality always been.

The realisation is close now, that the world you see does not create feelings of strife and fear but the exact opposite. The world you see is only a reflection of the strife and fear felt within.

The incoming raised energies give opportunity to see the world empowered by Love or deluded by fear. Due to the increased empowerment, the way the world is now perceived will be, therefore, either more and more beautiful or more and more terrifying, accordingly.

There is nothing outside you, only a projection of your mind as part of the One Mind.

*You are all perfect **now** in completeness and harmony and in reality you never left this. There **are** no fearful happenings, only images from the state of mind. The images projected at any moment of the day or night reflect whether the mind is following a fear thought or a Love thought and how deeply this is followed.*

These magnified energies now give the biggest opportunity to choose that there has ever been in the history of your perceived time. This choice to follow Love or follow thoughts of imperfection has never been more important.

This shift of mind is the dawning, which has been long awaited.

The reason your friend and every child of humanity walks the Earth at this particular time is because all are ripe for and catalysts for change, and all change will come from within."

Alice: "Higher Consciousness, I really want to be sure I am hearing you correctly. These words may be too painful for her, and I really want to help her."

Higher Consciousness: *"These words will undoubtedly be uncomfortable to the ego.*

Alice, do you not see? Your passion in wanting to help your friend is the same as hers in wanting to correct the world. You both perceive a need for healing. Do not her passions exactly reflect the passions you have long carried?

It is painful to the ego to give these passions away. Far surpassing the power of this passion, will a radiance of calmness ensue, which transcends all fear. Conflict will be felt no more, as it is just a dark reflection of conflict within. This can be gone in an instant if Love is chosen instead of fear.

What you 'see' as a physical world is but an illusion of strife projected from a frightened mind. There is another way of seeing.

*The Highest Consciousness within everyone is awaiting the choice. When **knowing Oneness** is reached, even for a fleeting moment, the illusion of imperfection will begin to dissolve. The beginnings of True Sight will be propagated in the warmth of Love.*

Your friend does not need healing. The world does not need healing.

All is well. All is Oneness, perfect in a perfect stream of consciousness; never beginning, never ending. So it is."

I made a snack of tea and hot toast and sat down to relax mind and body for ten minutes before meditation, but before I could drink or eat, an instant change of consciousness came over me and the connection was immediate. It felt instantly beautiful and I did not resist.

My hands involuntarily drifted up, **oh so slowly** to my face and removed my glasses more gently than I've **ever** done so myself. Something different was happening today.

Then my hands glided over my face and down my body in a slow cleansing, transforming movement which made me feel that a different and very beautiful presence was with me. This feeling was so gentle and so filled with Peace, time dissolved and each moment became eternity. I was aware in my mind of a golden cocoon becoming brighter all around my body.

I stated that it is my desire to become more and more receptive to Love Guidance and less and less receptive to ego thoughts, words and deeds, then surrendered again utterly and completely to Love and Light. I realised I did not have the spinning sensation that usually occurred when connecting, but instead I was experiencing a supreme calm, more profound than I have **ever** felt before. I sank deep into this calm, like a weary traveller into a warm pool.

Then, with an open heart, I softly repeated the words of my intent, and I felt a scintillating vibration, as of an electric current, rippling through me. Something was very different today.

I yielded to Supreme Love and stated, "I know nothing. Please guide me."

My hands were led in beautiful dance-like movements, oh so slowly, as I sat in ecstasy. My devious ego mind could bear this bliss no longer and had to divert me somehow and said in my mind, "You should not waste that tea and lovely hot toast." And in my weakness I glanced at the snack getting cold, but immediately pushed that thought out of my mind, gently asking, "What is happening today?"

Higher Consciousness: *"Your receptivity is opening more to us and there are transitions occurring. Due to your receptivity, you are feeling these transitions swiftly and profoundly."*

I felt as if I floated; held so lovingly, then my ego tempted me again and I thought of the slice of toast, showing my frailties and susceptibility to ego influence even in moments of bliss. I dismissed this diverting thought from my mind.

Higher Consciousness: "*Drink. It is not tea. Eat. It is not toast. It is Love and Light. The power of Love and Light is used to form every illusion. Absorb the Light as it receives Light from you. This is so and has always been so for all of creation. Everyday life and everyday objects will not divert you or be obstacles if they are seen as radiating the Love and Light that they are, and they can fulfil and magnify Truth.*

You are held within the power of The Spirit of God, which comes with Supreme Love to all. Welcome this power and you will be shown all things true. Fear not my children, all is well, all is safe and all will be revealed. Come to me in glorious Light and you will become beacons of Light.

We love you; every one and all, in the togetherness that you will feel more and more. This is just the beginning. Be ready for more of what you call change. You have taken your first kindergarten steps to knowing your connection to all.

You have totality now. It is in your grasp.

A wealth of Radiant Knowledge awaits your desire for Truth.

Let us help you to know this Truth.

Are you ready to accept what is yours?"

Do not feel alone

on your exciting journey

Visit my website and blog

w.w.w.findingthewayofpeace.com

And feel part of our community

INDEX